In Sickness and in Health

Brother's Pride

& Bahia

Two Ships. Two Fates. One Arrival Date.

Lyttelton Heads, 1863.

By Belinda Lansley

*Ancestral Journeys
of New Zealand
Series*

Without the help of the following people, this book would not have been possible. Special thanks to:

Al Smith, Boultenhouse Heritage Centre, Canada
Norton Wyse, Canadian Ship Historian
Greg Betzel, for the title suggestion, "In Sickness and in Health."
Marolyn Diver of Dornie Publishing for checking my cover design.
Shona C. Webb, for Walker family information and photo.
Merv Smith, for Smith family information and photo.
Lee Moake, for the Voice family information.
Phil Norton, for the photo of John Edward Hanson.
Grant Hay, for the Hay family information.
Margaret Gilmore, for the Scott family information.
Deb Donnell and family, for the Rountree family information.

Published by Belinda Lansley

Harewood, Christchurch
www.greatgrandmaswickerbasket.blogspot.co.nz

Original text © Belinda Lansley 2013
Images © named individuals, institutions
All rights reserved
ISBN 978-0-473-25016-4

Cover Design by Belinda Lansley
Cover Image: Port Lyttelton, 1863: *Illustrated London News* 17 Oct 1863

Dedicated to Stuie, Maia, Arielle and Louis

Belinda Lansley

Contents

Introduction	7
The Ships	9
The Voyage of the *Bahia*	25
Passengers on the *Bahia*	31
The Voyage of the *Brother's Pride*	33
Passengers on the *Brother's Pride*	69
Passenger Lists	85
Appendix	*105*
References	*116*

Introduction

While researching my ancestral ships, I came across an article about the horrific journey of the ship *Brother's Pride* and wanted to tell this story. This book covers the journey of the *Brother's Pride* and also the *Bahia*; ships that ferried new immigrants from Great Britain to New Zealand. As far as I know, this is the first time the whole story of the *Bahia* and *Brother's Pride* has been told in one place. The Voice family came out on this ship, and they married into the Pearce family I am related to! So, I do have a distant family connection to this immigrant ship.

This book has been a year in the making; delayed because of the Christchurch Earthquakes of 4 September 2010 and 22 February 2011, as most historical resources have been trapped in various buildings around Christchurch. I was waiting to obtain the J. P. Whitelaw notes from the Canterbury Museum, but decided I had sufficient information to publish without them. A second edition may include them.

All sources are referenced carefully at the back of this book. Some sources may have errors. Often in the past, people told exaggerated stories of their journey, or made incorrect entries in the records. Advertisements for ships often made a ship sound better than it really was in order to gain passengers, just as advertisements operate these days. So I have worked with what was available and hope this written record is as accurate as possible.

If anyone has further information on the ship's *Bahia* or *Brother's Pride* including ship diaries, family letters or comments in their family histories about the journey that they are willing to share, please contact me so it can be added to any future updated editions.

As a final note, I visited Camp Bay in 2013 to see if the rumour of a seat with a tribute to the *Brother's Pride* was correct. There is no such seat, but there is a big stone one for those buried at Camp Bay which says "Camp Bay Cemetery. In remembrance of the seventy prospective early settlers and sailors buried here between 1863–1877 when this area was a quarantine station." We can only be grateful that we do not have to suffer like our ancestors had to in those days.

Belinda Lansley

belinda.lansley@yahoo.co.nz

The Ships

On 22 July 1863, the *Bahia,* a 566 ton ship, left London bound for Lyttelton, New Zealand with 23 passengers. The next day, a 1236 ton ship, *Brother's Pride,* left London with 371 passengers on board, including many assisted immigrants. Both vessels took about 139 long and agonising days to reach the Heads of Lyttelton on 7 December 1863 due to bad weather, but the similarities ended there. One ship's voyage passed without event, while the other vessel became the ship of death, overcrowded with Government immigrants and with an incompetent crew.

Construction of the Ships

The *Bahia* was an English barque, built in 1857 in Sunderland, England by James Hardy.[1] It weighed 566 tons and had a burden of 1000 tons. The weight of burden was a good guide as to the maximum cargo allowed on board which would make the journey economic, as well as making sure the weight was not exceeded, which could cause the ship to sink while at sea.[2] The ship was sheathed in felt and yellow metal in 1862. It measured 138 feet long, 29 feet breadth, and 19 feet depth. The dimensions were a lot smaller than the *Brother's Pride* with the length being 40 feet shorter. The *Bahia* was often advertised in newspapers as a "clipper ship" due to the romanticism and perceived swift speed of a clipper, but actually the rigging of the sails would have made it technically a barque. A barque could have three or four masts mainly with square sails, but the aftermost had fore-and-aft sails.[3]

An unnamed example of a barque (Wikipedia)

The *Brother's Pride* was built in 1858 in Sackville, New Brunswick, Canada, by Christopher Boulthenhouse (c1802–1876). Christopher's father, Bedford Boultenhouse was a carpenter who had established a small shipyard at Wood Point near Sackville. Christopher built many ships. He started off constructing them at Wood Point like his father, and then moved his shipyard to Sackville in about 1840. Between 1840 and 1875 he built and launched forty-four vessels from his Sackville yard and in total constructed 60 vessels in this lifetime. He built the *Brother's Pride,* a 1236 ton ship, in 1858 and easily sold it to Saint John ship owner John Yeats, despite a downturn in the market at that time. In 1859 and 1860, however, Christopher had to deal with bankruptcy, due to hard times for ship builders, plus the tragedy of two sons dying. Christopher was, however, able to reopen a shipyard again in 1861 and built one or two vessels per year until 1866 and sporadically after that. Christopher died in 1876.[4]

C. Boultenhouse (courtesy Boultenhouse Heritage Centre)

Christopher's large house in Sackville now houses the Boultenhouse Heritage Centre, the only shipwright's house in New Brunswick to become a museum.[4]

The *Brother's Pride* was built using Birch, Tamarack, Spruce and Pitch Pine and fastened with iron bolts. In 1860 the ship was sheathed in felt and yellow metal. The dimensions of the ship were 179.8 feet long, 37.7 breadth and 22.55 feet deep. It had a weight of 1236 tons with a burden of 2500 tons.[5] *Brother's Pride* was launched on 26 June 1858.

The *Brother's Pride* was a clipper ship. The name "clipper ship" was a synonym for a merchant ship. They were first created by American ship builders in the 1840s and were extra fast, travelling on average 250 miles per day while other types of ships averaged 150 miles per day. English ship builders started to build them as well. They revolutionised sea transport and were wonderful ships to behold. Clipper ships had three masts and square sails, and it was this combination that made them so fast and popular in the 19th century.[2]

This generic picture of a clipper ship was in an advert for "Dr William's Pink Pills for Pale People", which was published in New Zealand newspapers in 1902. The ad mentions the Brother's Pride.[6]

The Names of the Ships

The ship *Bahia* was most likely named after one of the 26 states of Brazil, which was often visited by merchant ships. The word "Bahia" is an archaic spelling of the Portuguese word "baia" which means "bay,"[7] a very appropriate name for a ship. There is no documented proof, however.

One of the passengers of the *Brother's Pride*, H. B. Kirk, wrote a letter to the editor 30 years after the ship arrived in New Zealand. He stated that the ship was named by the owners, Messrs Miles Brothers. This is probably incorrect, as the ship was named on first registration in Canada and no owners called Messrs Miles Brothers have been found. The ship's name was spelt without the apostrophe on first registration in Canada, but once registered at Lloyds the apostrophe was added, causing it to be incorrectly named for the rest of its shipping career. Henry Brett's famous shipping book, *White Wings,* had the name with the apostrophe after the 's' meaning more than one brother, which was also incorrect. The original name is meant to be *Brothers Pride* but, because it was hardly ever spelt this way, the author has decided to spell it with the singular apostrophe.

Other ships called *Brother's Pride*

There was a barque called *Brother's Pride* of 379 tons, which was built in 1866 at McDonald's shipyard, Courtney Bay, St. John. New Brunswick, Canada. She was sailing at the same time as the clipper ship *Brother's Pride*. The barque was scuttled in the Gulf Stream near Florida on 7 May 1879 by the master, William Henry Tower. The Morning Post, 10

December 1881, mentions that a sailor on board heard the drilling of holes while going about his work on a voyage from Cuba. A couple of days later the ship was abandoned. He saw the Captain, First Mate and a sailor go back to the boat and the First Mate had an oil can in his hand. After they left, the ship was soon on fire. The crew all landed on the coast of Florida.

Captain Tower was put in Ludlow Street jail, New York, and had a huge bail of £25,000 over his head.

Owners of the Ships

The owner of the *Bahia* at the time of the 1863 journey was F. P. Wilson and the boat was registered to the Port of London. Willis, Gann and Co. chartered the boat to New Zealand in 1863.

The first owner of the *Brother's Pride* was John Yeats, who bought the ship off the builder, Christopher Boultenhouse.[8] On 2 November 1858, the ship was bought by Alfred Radcliffe and registered at Liverpool, England. There were other owners but the owner at the time of the 1863 journey to New Zealand was W & R Wright. Shaw, Savill & Co chartered the *Brother's Pride* from the owners in 1863.

Two Competing Companies

The *Brother's Pride* was one of Shaw, Savill & Co.'s line of packet ships and the *Bahia* was one of Willis, Gann & Co.'s packet ships. A packet ship was originally used for shipping post office mail to the colonies and other places around the world but this meaning was eventually extended to include passengers as well as mail.[9] Shaw, Savill & Co. and Willis, Gann & Co. advertised regularly in English newspapers, competing with each other for passengers.

NEW ZEALAND.—WILLIS, GANN, and Co.'s LINE.—The following clipper SHIPS are now rapidly loading, and will be the first despatched for the different ports:—

Ports.	Ships.	Tons.	Docks.	To Sail.
Canterbury	Bahia	1,000	London	July 15
Otago	Persian	2,000	London	July 20
Auckland	Green Jacket	2,500	London	July 25
Wellington	Bride	1,000	London	July 25
Canterbury	Zealandia	2,500	London	August 15

For freight or passage apply to Willis, Gann, and Co., 3, Crosby-sq.

CANTERBURY, New Zealand.—Notice.—Shippers and passengers are respectfully reminded that the first ship is the BAHIA, now rapidly filling up; to be followed by the ZEALANDIA, the favourite packet of the trade; both loading in the Shadwell-basin, London Docks.—Willis, Gann, and Co., 3, Crosby-square.

11 July 1863 The Times (London)

The Ships

In 1858, Robert Shaw and Walter Savill left Willis, Gann & Co., one of the leading companies sailing immigrants to New Zealand in the 1850s, and formed their own company called Shaw, Savill & Co. Shaw, Savill & Co. were to become one of the most well known and respected shipbrokers in the trade. The *Lord Ashley* was the first ship to sail from London on 28 May 1858. By 1865 the company had fifteen ship journeys running on the New Zealand service and in 1866 this increased to 68 ship voyages.[10]

In 1854 the provincial governments became responsible for immigration. The Province of Canterbury had the largest immigration scheme of all the provinces, bringing in almost a fifth of all immigrants between 1858 and 1870. Two thirds of all passengers arriving in Canterbury were assisted; generally, half of their fare paid by the Provincial Government.[11] The price for a steerage ticket was anywhere from £8 to £20, but on average most fares were around £13. In 1863 rival company Shaw, Savill & Co. secured the contract for carrying emigrants to Otago, the fares being £12 from Glasgow and £13 10s from London.[12] They had the majority of the market at this time. Shaw, Savill & Co had set the charges for passengers on the *Brother's Pride* in 1863 as follows:

Single man or woman	£13 6/
Couple	£26 12/
Child	£6 13/
Infant	free

The rates for cabin passengers on the *Bahia* are unknown as there is no original passenger list in existence. There is no mention of the cost for cabin passengers on either ship but for the *Clontarf* from 1855–57, Willis Gann were charging £60 for one person in a chief cabin measuring 6 by 7ft, or £40 each for two people. The second cabins were 6ft 9in by 7ft 6 in and for four people this cost £25 per person. Also available were second cabins for married couples measuring 3ft 6in by 7ft 8in at £25 per person.[13] It is likely the prices would have increased for cabin passengers in the 1860s.

The average annual wage for a housemaid in 1850s–1860s was from £11–£14[14] therefore the full cost of the journey was a full years wage. The average annual wage for a farm labourer in England and Wales in 1860 was £30 2s 4p[15], so the full cost of the journey was over a third of their annual wage. We can now see that travel to New Zealand was expensive and what a struggle it was to raise even half the fare. They often had help from family and friends already in the colony and of course the Provincial Government would assist by paying part of the fare.

"She will not Carry Government Assisted Emigrants"

The *Brother's Pride* and the *Bahia* were advertised in English newspapers to encourage people to use them for their passage to New Zealand. The advertisements for both ships were sometimes on the same day. Advertisements acted in the same way as our modern ads, with the truth being stretched somewhat to make a product or service sound better than it really was. The *Brother's Pride* advertised that it had "every modern appliance" including a water distilling apparatus to provide clean fresh water during the journey. The *Brother's Pride* advertisement claimed that, along with the *David G. Fleming*, "Being always loaded to a light draught of water, they offer to shippers a greater certainty of a smart passage and safe delivery of cargo than if filled up with cargo only."

> CANTERBURY direct.——The PASSENGERS' LINE.—Under Engagement with the Provincial Government.—The next ship is the BROTHER's PRIDE, A 1 2,500 tons, built in 1853, expressly for the passenger trade, and fitted with every modern appliance. She has a spacious poop, with state rooms much beyond the average dimensions, and very lofty between decks for second and third class; the arrangements for lighting and ventilation being quite equal to what are to be found in the chief saloon of ordinary ships. She is provided with a distilling apparatus, and provisioned and equipped on the improved scale, adopted by the Canterbury Government, which is acknowledged to be superior to anything hitherto adopted in the passenger trade. She will be succeeded by the famous packet David G. Fleming, A 1 3,060 tons, noted for her great speed, and in equipment not to be surpassed by any passenger ship afloat. These ships load in the East India Docks, and are despatched every three weeks, full or not full, with undeviating punctuality. Being always loaded to a light draught of water, they offer to shippers a greater certainty of a smart passage and safe delivery of cargo than if filled up with cargo only.—Shaw, Savill, and Co., 34, Leadenhall-street, London, E.O.
>
> CANTERBURY direct. —— The BROTHER's PRIDE, A 1, is loading rapidly in the East India Docks, and is guaranteed first ship.—Shaw, Savill, and Co., 34, Leadenhall-street, London, E.O.

11 July 1863 The Times (London)

These claims certainly didn't come true for the *Brother's Pride* voyage and, even though it wasn't loaded fully with cargo, it was certainly overloaded with passengers. The "fresh water" didn't stop the spread of disease on board and the "good ventilation" didn't seem to help either. In fact, the opposite was found in the *Brother's Pride* enquiry. The advertisement seems like a bit of a sham after what happened on board.

The advertisement for the *Bahia* also bent the truth slightly saying that the ship was a "clipper ship" when actually it was rigged as a barque. But the one advantage with the *Bahia* was that the ad stated, "she will not carry Government assisted emigrants." Because of this claim, the passengers who sailed on her were sure that a certain type of riff raff would not be sharing the journey with them. They probably would have paid a little more to have a comfortable passage with hopefully less of the lice, diseases and general loutish behaviour that often went with the poorer part of society. They would also avoid the possibility of overcrowding. This extra money, to ensure a safe and comfortable journey, paid off for these passengers as we will see later on.

The Captain, P. Le Fanu, was named as "a gentleman of acknowledged popularity" and maybe this was also the reason for the success of the voyage, being a more upstanding individual than the Captain of the *Brother's Pride*, who comes across in the records as stubborn, lacking discipline and generally flouting the law.

> CANTERBURY, New Zealand.—WILLIS, GANN, and Co's LINE.—To follow the Zambesi and sail punctually on the 8th July, the beautiful clipper BAHIA, A 1 11 years, 565 tons register, 1,000 tons burden, P. Le FANU, Commander; now loading in the London Docks. This fine, high-classed ship has most superior accommodations for passengers, and is commanded by a gentleman of acknowleged popularity. She will be despatched with the unvarying punctuality observed in this line, and offers an opportunity unsurpassed by any other now before the public. She will not carry Government assisted emigrants.—Willis, Gann, and Co., 3, Crosby-square, E.C.

6 June 1863 The Times (London)

Life on Board a Clipper Ship

The Willis, Gann & Co. chart from the 1855–1857 period, on the following page, shows the food allocated to the different classes of passengers.[13] Shaw, Savill and Co. would have probably had a similar chart with similar food items for passengers. The second cabin and steerage passengers were the only ones who received lime juice to keep away the scurvy. Maybe the first class passengers received enough vitamin C from the extra muscatel raisins and preserved carrots that were served to them. Records show that there were usually fowl in coups to produce eggs and meat, and sometimes larger animals for fresh meat. Water was stored in barrels, and became stale and often grew algae or had vermin fall in and die. Food was stored in lidded barrels but if someone left the lid off they could often become contaminated with rat and mice droppings. The bad hygiene often led to dysentery, cholera and many deaths on board. Flour often had weevils.

Illness was rife on some journeys, especially when steerage passengers were confined below decks during massive storms in the Southern Ocean. The ships were cleaned with vinegar and chloride of lime to remove vomit and make things smell better, while precious water was kept for drinking.

WEEKLY DIETARY SCALE FOR EACH ADULT PASSENGER.

Articles.	Chief Cabin.	Second Cabin.	Steerage.
Preserved Meats	1½ lb.	1½ lb.	1 lb.
Preserved Salmon	½ "	—	—
Assorted Soups	1 "	—	—
Soup and Bouilli	—	½ lb.	—
York Ham	1 "	½ "	—
Tripe	½ "	—	—
Fish	½ "	¼ lb.	—
Prime India Beef	½ "	1 "	1¼ lb.
Irish Mess Pork	1 "	1½ "	1 "
Biscuit	3 "	4¼ "	3½ "
Flour	4¼ "	4¼ "	3 "
Rice	1 "	1 "	½ "
Barley	¼ "	½ "	—
Peas	½ pint	½ pint	½ pint
Oatmeal	½ "	½ "	1 "
Preserved Milk	½ "	—	—
Sugar, refined	¾ lb.	—	—
Sugar, raw	¼ "	1 lb.	1 lb.
Lime Juice	—	6 oz.	6 oz.
Tea	3 oz.	1½ oz.	1½ oz.
Coffee	5 "	3 "	2 "
Butter	½ lb.	½ lb.	6 "
Cheese	½ "	¼ "	—
Currants	¼ "	¼ "	—
Raisins, Valentia	½ "	½ "	½ lb.
Raisins, Muscatel	¼ "	—	—
Suet	½ "	6 oz.	6 oz.
Preserved Carrots	½ "	—	—
Pickles	¼ pint	¼ pint	¼ pint
Vinegar	¼ "	—	—
Mustard	½ oz.	½ oz.	½ oz.
Pepper	½ "	¼ "	¼ "
Salt	2 "	2 "	2 "
Potatoes, fresh or	3½ lb.	3½ lb.	2 lb.
Preserved ditto	½ "	½ "	½ "
Water	28 quarts	21 quarts	21 quarts

Food chart for Willis, Gann and Co. from 1855–1857

There was an advertisement in the Christchurch *Press* dated 28 January 1864 selling surplus stores ex-*Brother's Pride*. This included "the usual assortment of Ship's Stores." One would hope that these items were still fresh and safe to eat after a 139-day journey.

Auction Sales.

UNRESERVED SALE
OF
SURPLUS STORES EX BROTHERS PRIDE

THURSDAY, 28TH INSTANT.

MR. LOUISSON is instructed by Messrs. J. T. Peacock & Co. to have sold at their Stores, Lyttelton,

BY AUCTION WITHOUT RESERVE,

on Thursday next, the 28th inst., the whole of the Surplus Stores ex Brother's Pride,

CONSISTING OF
Pork
Preserved meats
Bread
Rice
Sugar
Tea
Pickles
Lime juice
Preserved potatoes
Peas
Mustard

And the usual assortment of Ship's Stores.

Iron tanks
Water casks
Ship's fittings
&c., &c.

Terms at Sale.

Sale at 1 o'clock.

Press 28 January 1864

Toileting on ships was not pleasant. Often, pieces of rag, soaked in vinegar, were hung on the back of the toilet door. These were used to wipe with and were shared over and over, often leading to dysentery! The sewage was often flushed into the bilge with buckets of water until emptied at port. The bilge was below steerage so the stench was not pleasant. People would be horrified these days, but back then hygiene was generally not understood.[16]

The Ships

Married couples' accommodation in steerage: bunks to the left and right; central table; light from the uncovered hatch. (London Illustrated News, 13 April 1844)

The sleeping arrangements were bunk beds for steerage, with single women and single men having their own areas. Families often became separated as, most of the time, children over the age of 12 were transferred to the single men's or single women's quarters. Bedding was aired in fine weather but often became soaked if water came into the ship and this led to influenza and pneumonia outbreaks.[16]

Some ships were better managed than others. The *Bahia* was, it seems, a well managed ship with low passenger numbers and no illness reported. The tragic death count on the *Brother's Pride* suggests poor management, also bad weather and bad luck that major outbreaks of illness took hold. Even before leaving port the illness had been spread by a young boy who was taken off the ship. An enquiry was held and many mistakes found. More about the ill-fated ship can be read in the journey summary.

On the more positive side, a ship journey such as this would have been one of life's biggest adventures for the migrants. They would see and experience things they never dreamed of, including strange sea creatures, new constellations in the skies and a sea voyage that most would never repeat again in their lifetime, culminating in a strange new land at the final port. At night, the passengers entertained each other with music, lectures of the new country and games, made new friends and contacts and looked forward to a brighter future in their new country.

Crew of a Clipper Ship

The average crew of a clipper ship without migrants was about 17, including the Captain, First Mate (or Chief Officer), Second Mate, Midshipman (Apprentice Officer), Ship's Carpenter, Boatswain, 9-10 ordinary seamen and the Cabin Boy, who was used for mundane duties. There were usually two cooks: the Passenger's Cook, who made food for the steerage passengers, and the Ship's Cook for the cabin passengers and crew, who catered for their more refined tastes.

The crew numbers became closer to 40 when emigrants were on board, with additional crew including the Ship's Surgeon and Constable to keep the passenger welfare attended to. A Schoolmaster was on board, to teach the children, and a Matron, to separate the single woman from the single men. Sometimes there was a Minister on board. There were usually several Stewards, who looked after the Cabin Passengers. Some people took up a job on board to get free passage out.[17] The Matron was often a woman looking to emigrate, who took on the job in exchange for free passage.

Wages for the crew were on average £7 per month on the way to New Zealand, with good food and comfortable accommodation, but up to a £100 wage for the home journey, to ensure crew stuck with the ship and didn't desert once in New Zealand. Even with the better wage, desertions were common.[17]

Clipper Ship (Illustrated London News, 18 October 1851)

The Ships

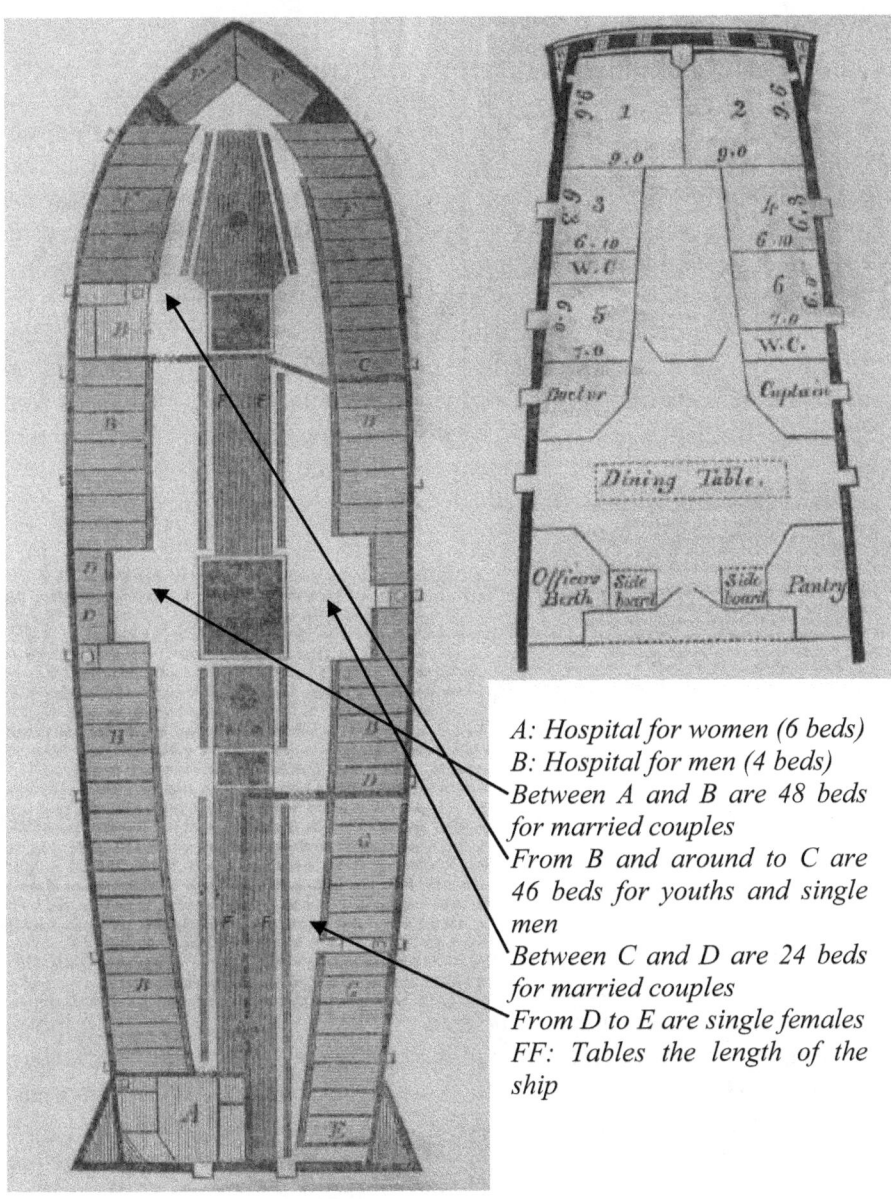

A: Hospital for women (6 beds)
B: Hospital for men (4 beds)
Between A and B are 48 beds for married couples
From B and around to C are 46 beds for youths and single men
Between C and D are 24 beds for married couples
From D to E are single females
FF: Tables the length of the ship

Plan of Emigrant Ship Between Decks (left) and Plan of Cabin Accommodation (right) (courtesy London Illustrated News)

Other Australasian Journeys for the ships

After the trip to New Zealand, the *Bahia*, of Scarborough, made a journey from London to Sydney, arriving 26 June 1865 under the command of Samuel Halliday Smith. It was detained in the Channel for a whole month—a very long time indeed—and didn't pass the Lizard (a peninsula in South Cornwall) until 3 March. The *Bahia* crossed the equator on 1 April and reached the meridian of the Cape of Good Hope on 14 May. The journey was then extremely fast to the S.W. Cape of Van Diemen's Land (Tasmania), which they rounded on 17 June. She sailed, or as the papers put it "ran her easting," in the latitudes of 41°S and 44°S. The winds were prevailing from N.E. to N.N.W., with very fine weather. There was no passenger list printed in the newspapers.[18] While the ship was in port, two sailors, Frank Miller and Daniel Carmichael, were convicted of desertion and sentenced to six weeks hard labour in jail.[19]

The *Brother's Pride* made another journey from London to Australasia, arriving 26 July 1865 at Port Phillip Heads, Melbourne, Australia.[20] They arrived into Hobson's Bay on 27 July with seven cabin passengers (unnamed in the newspaper) and cargo. The Captain was H. Welsh. Captain Glendinning, from the New Zealand voyage 18 months earlier, was no longer in charge.[21]

While the ship was discharging cargo at Hobson's Bay railway pier, Donald McGregor, boatswain of the *Brother's Pride,* was charged with indecent behaviour in a public place. He was found underneath the railway pier at 5pm on a Sunday, looking up between the crevices in the planks. Ladies would have been walking along in large dresses. The Captain had promoted Donald to boatswain on arrival at Melbourne for his good conduct during the voyage out and said that he would pay any fine imposed on Donald. Donald said he had gone under the pier "for necessary purpose." He was fined £5 with consideration taken for his ignorance regarding previous offences under the same railway pier. The chinks had already been boarded up, but someone had pulled the boards up. The pier had become an unsavoury place to walk.[22]

The *Brother's Pride* sailed for Callao on 1 September 1865. Callao was the centre of the guano trade. A load of guano would make the journey back to the United Kingdom more economic for the ship owners.[23]

The Demise of two ships

The *Bahia* appears in the 1875 Lloyds directory of shipping in the United Kingdom and then disappears from the records. She may have become French owned, as there was a suggestion in the British newspapers of a French owned ship called *Bahia*, or she may have been wrecked. What her final fate was, we can only guess at.

The *Brother's Pride* departed London on 20 June 1877 for Sydney, Australia.[24] This was her last journey. According to records in America, the *Brother's Pride* foundered off Cape Seal near the Cape of Good Hope, South Africa and the Register for this ship closed on 16 July 1877.[25] It appears that the boat got into trouble rounding the Cape on the way to Sydney. There was never a report in the newspapers of the *Brother's Pride* arriving in Sydney and all ships were usually reported. After extensive research, nothing more can be found about the ship's demise.

Shipwreck. *(Illustrated London News, 10 June 1843.)*

The Voyage of the Bahia
(22 July 1863 – 7 December 1863)

The *Bahia* was a fine barque, which departed London on 22 July 1863, the day before the *Brother's Pride*. The *Press* of 9 December 1863 had a short summary of the voyage of the *Bahia* as follows:

"The *Bahia*.—The ship *Bahia*, 566 tons, commanded by Captain Le Fann [Fanu], anchored off Rhodes' Bay [now Purau Bay] on Monday morning at 10 a.m. 137 days out. She sailed from the Downs on 26th July, experienced light and contrary winds to the line, which was crossed on the 19th September. She experienced moderate weather and calms to the longitude of the Cape, and from 30 degrees east to Van Diemen's Land she had very bad weather, the barometer ranging from 28.30 to 28.70 for 30 days, during which at times it blew perfect hurricanes. She brings several cabin passengers and a valuable cargo."[26]

There isn't much more to be found for this journey. Even though they had difficulties at sea, the same as the *Brother's Pride*, all passengers and crew were alive and healthy on arrival at the Port of Lyttelton. The first part of the journey was uneventful, but having a whole month of bad weather must have taken its toll on the passengers somewhat and one can imagine that the boredom on board would have been great. Often passengers were battened down inside the ship for days and weeks on end.

Such a small newspaper report can only mean good news. There was nothing tragic or distressing of note during the voyage.

Captain Le Fanu's name appears in the Lloyd's Register. His name is incorrectly spelt in New Zealand newspapers, however, as Le Fann and even appears as Le Farm at one point.

SHIP "BAHIA" FROM LONDON.

THE Captain and Agents will not be responsible for any debts contracted by the Crew of the Ship.

6318   LE FARM.

Lyttelton Times, 15 December 1863

Bahia Cargo 1863

In the Bahia, Peacock & Co., agents: 2 cases, 1 box, Tipping; 33,300 slates, 3 cases, Aikman, Knight & Co; 1 pkg apparel, Wishart; 25 hhds vinegar, 100 casks cement, 11 hhds, 21 qr casks, 276 cases, 20 crates, 14 casks 10 bales, 350 boxes, 84 cases, 66 casks whiting, 300 bags, 137 cases, 15 do, 2 casks, 4 bdls, 12 brls, 77 bales tobacco, 13 bales, 854 deals, 191 bags salt, 20 water casks, Dalgety, Buckley & Co; 1 case sundries, Carte; 1 pkg, Robinson; 6 casks hardware, 1 case grates, Hawkes & Strouts; 5 cases, England Bros; 6 qr casks whiskey, 40 hhds ale, 10 kilderkins do, 6 casks, 7 cases, 2 chests, 1 cask, 9 cases, 2 jars, 1 cask, 4 bags, 1 dog and kennel, 3 cases, 46 bdl wire, 40 kegs white lead, 50 drums oil, 50 casks beer, 4 bales paper, 1 case effects, 1 case cart and harness; 100 tons coals, 40 cases, 200 bdls wire, Order; 1 box, Beeby; 1 case, C. Dangerenne; 1 do, J. Wylde; 3 cases, Wingate & Middleton; 7 pkgs, 36 pieces iron, 108 bdls do, 13 do sash bars, 30 do iron wire, 5 hhd, 6 casks, 2 cases, 10 bundles spades, 11 cases, 1 tub, 7 crates, 6 boxes tin plates, 8 rollers, 4 bdls handles, 1 case ditto, 1 bale scythe ditto, Reece & Co.; 22 bales paper, FitzGerald; 4 cases, 2 casks sundries, J. D. Macpherson; 5 cases, Walker; 2 casks seeds, Mounsey; 2 casks, Deamer; 100 cases old tom, 70 cases brandy, 2 hhds old tom, 2 hhds brandy, 39 qr-casks ditto, 2 hhds rum, Dann & Bishop; 1 cask chain, 6 cases, 3 pkgs, 1 case, 100 casks beer, Renshaw; 2 cases ironwire, 1 cask earthenware, 115 boxes candles, 8 cases tapers, 10 casks rice, 2 ditto rock salt, 2 ditto saltpetre, 2 ditto carbonate soda, 1 ditto whiting, 5 barrels soda, 1 case chemicals, 2 casks coffee, 6 ditto herrings, 3 ditto sardines, 4 ditto blacking, 1 case, 1 bale candle cotton, 1 keg sausage skins, 66 cases oilmen's stores, 1 case clocks, 2 pkgs brushware, 2 bales covers, 1 ditto plough lines, 80 bags salt, 2 casks pearl barley, 1 ditto carraways, 1 ditto split peas, 2 ditto arrowroot, 3 boxes sago, 1 barrel tapioca, 2 ditto oatmeal, 1 ditto ginger, 1 ditto cocoa, 2 cases figs, 4 bags pepper, 2 hogsheads ironmongery, 15 bundles, 2 cases glassware, 1 cask crockeryware, 5 bdls forks, 1 hhd bellows, 2 cases, 2 casks ironware, 1 hhd brackets, 3 halftierces tobacco, 30 camp ovens and covers, 1 brl ginger, 1 bag coffee, 7 hhds wine, 10 qr-casks, 40 cases, 8 hhds spirits, 3 brls, 12 qr-casks, 95 cases, 40 hhds beer, 5 cases vinegar, 1 do blue, 6 do mustard, 9 do starch, 1 hhd sugar, Gould & Miles; 7 casks, 23 cases, 34 kegs, 2 machines, 3 boxes, 2 rolls, 15 bdls, Reed; 3 cases, Looke & Co; 1 case, Strouts; 1 case, C. Blakiston; 25 kegs, 10 cases, 1 tierce, 3 casks, Booth; 9 cases, 4 bales, D. Clarkson; 1 case seeds, 1 case, 8 rollers, 4 bdls handles, Reece & Hislop; 1 case, Enys; 1 box, Ellice; 60 casks bottled beer, Heywood & Co; 1 case, Fletcher; 1 case, Field; 1 box, Raine; 2 cases, 2 casks, McKellar; 1 case saddlery, LeCren; 31 bales, Lance: 52 cases brandy, 60 casks bottled ale, 6 qr-casks gin, 50 boxes candles, 6 qr-casks rum, 24 cases sherry, 24 cases port, 12 cases champagne, 5 cases coffee, 6 qr-casks whiskey, 10 casks sodawater and lemonade, 1 case tobacco pipes, 100 bdls fencing wire, 120 standards, Beswick & Birch; 42 bdls wire, 2 bales woolpacks, 1 case apparel, 12 trunks boots, 3 bales blankets, 41 barrels, 107 barrels sugar, 7 pkgs groceries, 2 pockets hops, 6 barrels currants, 5 brls raisins, 2 brls muscatels, Peacock & Co.; 8 cases iron, 10 crates, 2 hhds, 22 casks, 1,522 bars iron, Anderson; 38 pkgs, Goodman; 1 box, Stancil; 7 cases, 5 casks, 3 bags, 18 bales, 4 pkgs, 2 barrels, J. K. Wilson; 1 case, Pilbrow; 1 case, 40 boxes, Miles & Co.; 1 box, Jackson; 1 case, Harman; 1 case, Cookson & Co.; 6 boxes tin plates, Hitch; 2 hhds ale, Hargreaves & Co.; 3 hhds tobacco, 6 pkgs spirits tar, Rhodes.

List of cargo on board the Bahia, Lyttelton Times 10 December 1863

Map of the Journey of the *Bahia*

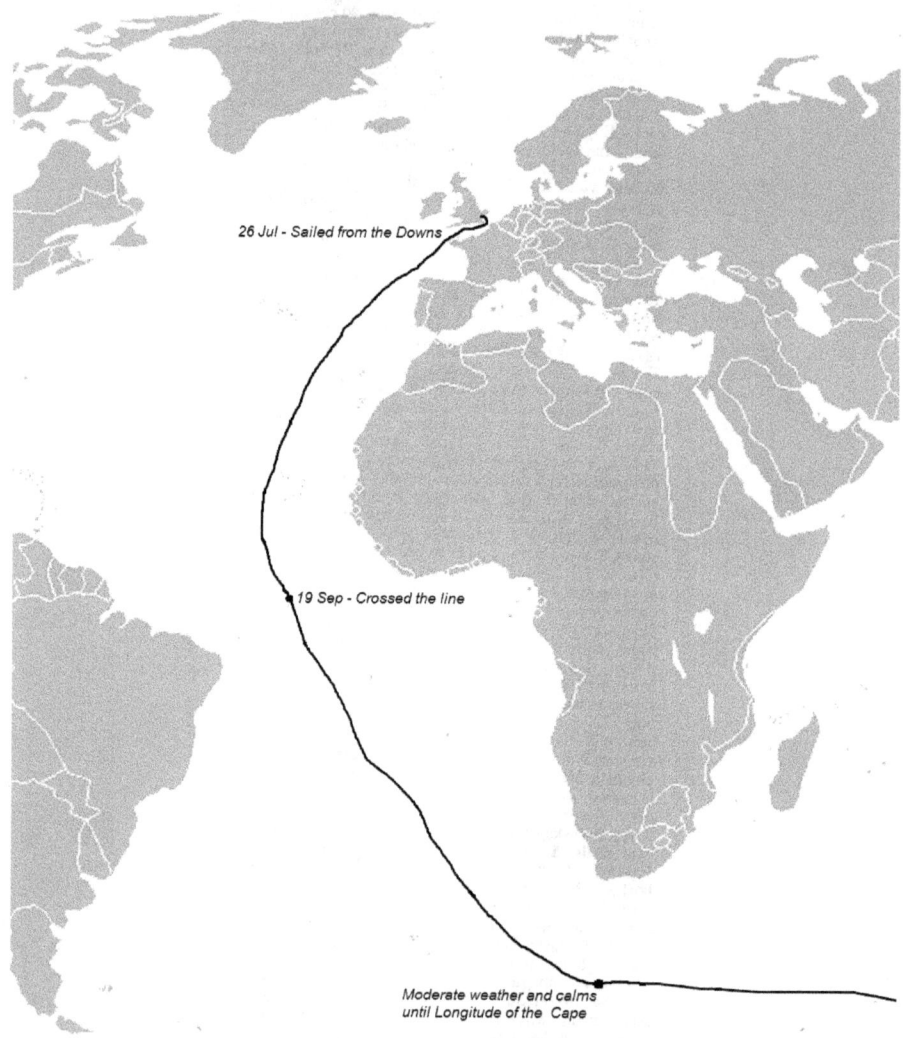

The Voyage of the *Bahia*

(22 July 1863 – 7 December 1863)

Passengers on the Bahia

Passengers on the *Bahia*

Cambridge

John Miles Cambridge was born in Norfolk, England, in about 1845, and travelled to New Zealand on the ship *Bahia*. He lived in Lyttelton and then Kaiapoi for a while before starting a chemist business in Ashburton in 1873. He was a keen sportsman, was really into fishing and was a member of the Acclimatisation Society. He was a Master of the Somerset Masonic Lodge and an officer of the Kilwinning Loyal Arch Chapter and also an Officer of the Grand Lodge (English Constitution). He was heavily involved in the St Stephen's Anglican Church.[27] John married Mary Jane Middleweek in 1867.[28] Mary was a reclusive person and an invalid for many years before she died in Ashburton in 1902.[29] John married again in 1903 to Elizabeth Hocken Rundle.[28] On John's death he left a widow and four children by his second wife and a daughter and four sons by his first wife. He died on 3 October 1918 in Ashburton.[30]

Ross

John Ross was from Helmsdale, Scotland, and travelled to New Zealand on the *Bahia* after being appointed as a school teacher at the Presbyterian Church School, Lyttelton. He was recruited to assist Mr. Fergusson, who was teaching there.[31] John taught there for ten years. The Ross family lived at Lyttelton and their daughter Jeanie married at her parents' house in 1901.[32] John retired in 1902 from the Lyttelton Borough School and was presented with a Gladstone Bag and a silver teapot.[33] He had worked there for 28 years. He died of an apoplectic stroke on 17 November 1902, only a few months after retiring. The flags at his local school were raised half mast as a mark of respect. He left a grown up family.[34]

The Voyage of the Brother's Pride
(23 July 1863 – 9 December 1863)

The Voyage of the *Brother's Pride* 1863

Newspapers mention that the *Brother's Pride* was loading for New Zealand with the captain Radcliffe.[35] On arrival in New Zealand, the captain was actually Captain Glendinning. Radcliffe was the owner of the ship. Did he choose Glendinning at the last minute or was it just an error in the newspaper? Would a different Captain have changed the outcome of this voyage? We can only guess at this.[36]

There were two accounts from passengers for this journey, by H. B. Kirk and John Whitelaw. Also, the enquiry gives lots of statements from passengers and the Doctor as to what happened on board.

The *Brother's Pride* left London on 23 July 1863 and arrived at Gravesend that day.[37] According to the ship's Doctor Fitzherbert Dermott the passengers were "mustered" in Gravesend on 24 July 1863. They had medical checks before boarding the ship. One unnamed boy, aged seven, was found to have scarlet fever and was sent ashore. He travelled back to his home in Gloucestershire and died three days later. The boat left Gravesend on 26 July, nobody realising that the scarlet fever had already been transmitted among the passengers.[38] This was the beginning of a hellish journey for the passengers and crew, but at that time the passengers were enjoying the view of the gorgeous towns of Dover and Folkstone and the white cliffs of Albion, quite oblivious to what was ahead of them in the coming months. Scottish captain Alexander Glendinning was at the helm and everyone was happy.[37]

On 27 July, the ship passed Hastings and Beachy Head and by evening lost sight of the Isle of Wight and the Coast of France. On 1 August, nearly everyone on the ship was sea sick.[37]

It was only a few days after leaving Gravesend when a large number of the children came down with scarlet fever. At this stage of the journey, most recovered from the disease.[38] On 4 August the first child was born on board.[37] However, the happiness of this event was shattered when a child died[38] the next day of scarlet fever. Joseph Bailey was 2 years and 9 months old.[39] On the same day, a bouilli soup tin exploded and caused a bit of excitement on board.[37]

Sometime in August, they met the ship *Mayflower* travelling from Liverpool to Falmouth. The *Mayflower* indicated they would send letters back home, so everyone on the *Brother's Pride* ran around looking for pens, ink and paper. There was a lot of silence as people wrote quickly and a bag of letters was taken in one of the ship's boats to the *Mayflower*.

Typhus was the next disease to hit the ship and started at the latitude of about 30 to 40° N. On board were a large number of people from the Forest of Dean, Gloucestershire; a mining area. For some reason the typhus hit this group of people and hardly any of the other passengers. This disease proved fatal to many. The Gloucestershire passengers had their bunks near to the main hatch which meant their quarters should have been well ventilated, and therefore disease less likely.[38] Epidemic typhus was often spread by lice on humans and was highly contagious, especially in dark enclosed spaces with lots of humans present. Ships were the perfect breeding ground. Symptoms included high fever, rash, severe muscle pains, chills and severe headaches, often resulting in death.[40]

During the days of illness "time would have pressed very heavily" on the passengers if it weren't for the light-hearted friendly spirited guys on board, such as Mr Torrens and Mr Hanson as well as a few others.[37]

They sighted one of the Madeira Islands, Porto Santo, on 17 August and a couple of days later on 20 August an unnamed passenger sold his wife. She was considered worth only £5, and the husband was knocked down at this figure. Her husband must have been insane, as his eventual home in Christchurch was the Sunnyside Asylum.[37]

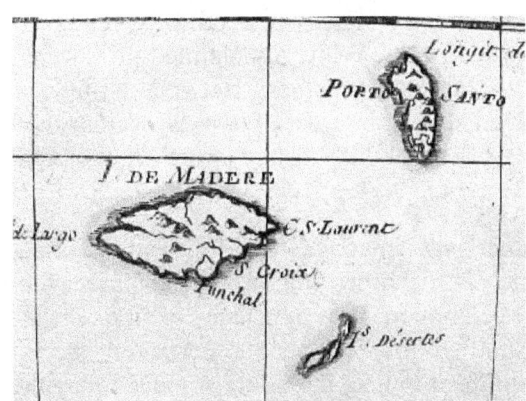

A map showing the island of Porto Santo

On 6 September the ship was at about latitude 4.12°. The *Brother's Pride* spoke another ship and gained some live pigs. The pigs were put in the pen, which at that stage held the sheep, and the sheep were then allowed to run loose around the deck, defecating everywhere.[41]

By 9 September there had been five births and nine deaths. And on 13 September they were sailing next to the ship *Herbert* of Boston. It was sailing from Cardiff, South Wales, to the Cape of Good Hope.[37]

On 16 September, they crossed the equator and the passengers had a lot of fun and "good natured chaff" according to H. B. Kirk, who was remembering the voyage 30 years later.[37] However, John Whitelaw stated about a month after arriving in Lyttelton that on 17 September they crossed the line and that the wives and children panicked. A dozen of Captain Glendinning's men ran through the 'tween decks with their faces blackened and a canvas batten, blackmailing the passengers for drinking money. If the passengers didn't pay, they got "shaved." The passengers were angry at the unfairness of this, but there was also a kind of excitement at the same time.[42] The "shaving" process involved tar being put on the face and then "shaved" off with iron – certainly not a pleasant experience for anyone. People were also "swilled" in a sail full of water after the shaving was finished.[43] Most people paid the money to the loutish sailors but a few were forced to get shaved. Captain Glendinning permitted this to happen and "patronised" it, according to John Whitelaw. Even Dr. Dermott "frowned on and stigmatized a few who resisted, assuring them he would not fail to remember them for so doing."[42]

According to the doctor of the ship, Fitzherbert Dermott, the fever was "truly of an appalling character" at around the latitude of 8 to 12° S, causing panic in the passengers. According to the Doctor, passengers that were panicking about the illnesses seemed to be the ones who then caught the fever.[38] However, John Whitelaw claimed they were at this latitude at around the 22nd to 24th of September. Between latitude 3 and 27° S, there were only two deaths, at an interval of two days, from the "appalling" fever that the Doctor talked about. They were in these latitudes from 12 September to 3 October.[42]

John said the panic was "imaginary" and the only panic had been from the shaving incident. John claimed that on 23 September the passengers were all happy and celebrated the marriage of the second mate to Jane McWilliam, a Scottish girl.[42] After the ceremony there was dancing and singing and all kinds of music, including someone playing bagpipes. H. B. Kirk called them "the dreadful bagpipes." They had three ships nearby, travelling from England to the Cape and Bombay. The passengers bathed in the sea as it was calm due to the fact there was no wind. They generally had a lovely time![37]

On 1 October the ship had a regular cleaning and a fresh set of sails was hoisted. The passengers joy was broken, however, when Sophia Rosser died, leaving her son Charles an orphan, his father having died earlier in the voyage. H. B. Kirk said he was only 12 to 18 months old and how he and many of the other passengers had no idea what became of him and wanted to know and to meet him (this was in 1893). Charles' fate is discussed further on in this book.[37]

The weather near the Equator was sometimes sultry and oppressive. According to Dermott, the crew made sure the boat was clean and disinfectants were constantly used - the 'tween decks, as they were called, well ventilated and the wind sails constantly down.[38] The enquiry after arrival uncovered a different story.

The *Brother's Pride* caught a light wind which took it further south and the health of the passengers seemed to improve somewhat. There was still a long way to travel and the ship was only now in the latitude of the Cape of Good Hope. Dr Dermott and Captain Glendinning decided to take the ship into the Cape of Good Hope to pick up more medical supplies and some fresh vegetables and meat. They also wanted to pick up wine and brandy, which were seen as a necessary medicine for the sick.[38] The passengers probably thought that alcohol was a definite necessity on a horrifically long and painful ship voyage! Even the Doctor was seen worse for drink.

The ship arrived at Cape Town on the 84th day out from London, or more specifically 18 October 1863. They had endured 14 deaths so far, four adults and ten children, only about a quarter of the final 46 deaths. If only they knew what was to come, many of the passengers may have jumped ship to escape the horror.

H. B. Kirk painted an interesting picture of their time in Cape Town. He described the houses as "low and white" and that Cape Town had "decent" public buildings and large Botanical Gardens. The American Confederate steamer *Alabama*, with Captain Semmes in charge, had been in the harbour just before *Brother's Pride* arrived. Captain Wilkes was commanding the paddle steamer *Vanderbilt,* a North American man of war that had been given instructions to capture the *Alabama*. The large and rather scary steamer was waiting outside the harbour for the *Alabama*. However the *Alabama* escaped in some heavy fog past the *Vanderbilt*. The *Vanderbilt* came into harbour the next day to look for the other ship but soon realised they had left. The passengers of the *Brother's Pride* saw this large ship and were relieved there was no conflict in the harbour. However they were probably a little disappointed not to have seen the *Alabama*, which had almost been the cause of a public holiday in Cape Town.

The *Alabama* had such a reputation that every man, woman and child wanted to go on board, or even just catch a glimpse of it. The *Alabama* had captured many American ships and often set them on fire or sunk them. Captain Semmes was considered to be quite cruel, and used torture on his prisoners. He was considered a pirate when he was finally arrested in Alabama in 1865.[44]

Captain Raphael Semmes (front) and First Lieutenant John Kell on the CSS Alabama, Cape Town, August 1863 — only two months before the Brother's Pride arrived in harbour. Captain Semmes is standing next to his ship's 110-pounder rifled gun. (Creative Commons Attr. Licence 3.0).

The US paddle steamer USS Valderbilt, 1862 (Creative Commons Attribution Licence 3.0)

According to the Doctor, all the passengers went on shore, except for about four to six who stayed on the ship.[38] This was on 19 October 1863.[37] However, John Whitelaw claimed the Doctor's statement was incorrect and that many passengers were still on board and never left the ship.[42]

The Doctor said they stayed for three days in Cape Town[38] (John Whitelaw said four days[42]) and fulfilled all the necessities for the journey to New Zealand, with the passengers being happy and maybe relieved to be on land.[38] John Whitelaw stated that the 2lbs. meat and 2 dozen potatoes that were bought for each adult were exhausted while they were still at the Cape and during the subsequent voyage – not lasting long at all and maybe having very little effect on improving the health of the passengers.[42] This stop apparently added three extra weeks to the journey![41]

Cape Town, 1834. (Creative Commons Attribution Licence 3.0)

The *Brother's Pride* left Cape Town on 22 October. They sailed around Robin Island, down the harbour and off to New Zealand.[37] At the Cape, the ship had gained 6 live sheep and a goat, which were also kept loose making the boards of the deck absolutely filthy.[41] They also gained approximately 16 "stowaways" from the Cape, who boarded by watermen taking them to the side of the boat. These men were only noticed by the Captain three days out from Cape Town.[45]

Four days after leaving port, a thirteen year old boy, John Ellery, became infected with Scarlatina Maligna which is an acute and usually lethal form of scarlet fever. He was a second cabin passenger, son of Mrs Ellery, and according to the surgeon "a fine boy." Even though he was a strong healthy boy, he died tragically of this disease on 2 November 1863; suffocating to death.[38] The Ellery family are not listed as there is only a passenger list for steerage.[39] Because of the close confines of the ship, this disease spread rapidly and easily, causing the whole ship to be like a hospital.[38]

The vision of what happened next is almost too hard to imagine. Children would seem healthy one minute and then be dead within just a few hours, dying of suffocation.[38] Parents would have been crying, screaming, praying for their children, to no avail. Nearly whole families were wiped out during this voyage. Funerals on ships were often done in the early morning with the body wrapped in sails and weighted with chain and placed on a board, a Union Jack flag draped over the top. Then the board would be placed on the edge of the ship while the ceremony was taking place and the body was then slid into the sea, to the wails of the family.[46]

The worst effected family on the trip was the Brown family who lost Mrs Janet Brown and four children including a two week old baby boy who was born on the ship. Only the father, John, and one daughter, Margaret, aged 5, were left. On the other hand, the Round family had two parents and seven children on board and all survived. A lucky family indeed![47]

On 11 November, the *Brother's Pride* passed Amsterdam Isle and two days later encountered terrible weather and rough seas. On 14 November, it was very stormy and the Doctor ordered the hatches to be battened down. He seemed very drunk that night and many of the passengers noticed this.[41] By 17 November there had been 31 deaths. Mr Torrens and Mr Kirk used a coffee mill to grind coarse oatmeal into a fine gruel so that it could be eaten more easily by the sick,[37] and by 19 November all provisions for the sick had run out, apart from gin.[41]

On 25 November, they encountered fog, the first they had seen since they left England. On 5 December, the Doctor could not keep his balance while attending Mrs Mason for a miscarriage and fell into the bunk where she was lying. He smelt of gin according to John Mason. The Doctor seemed to have been drunk on a few occasions but not everyone noticed this.[41]

They finally saw New Zealand on 6 December according to H. B. Kirk. The *Bahia* was creeping up the New Zealand coast with them. She had left the day before them on 22 July 1863 and encountered the same bad sailing conditions.[37]

Typhus fever was still rampant on the ship. The diseases didn't let up and were still present when the ship reached the Port of Lyttelton.[38] There were also rumours of immorality and bad ship management.

Fitzherbert Dermott's letter to the Editor of the *Press* dated 29 December 1863 ended with the following statement from him, showing how worn out he was:

"This condition of things existed, more or less, until we neared this shore, long before doing so I had frequently expressed the opinion and also the wish that, on our arrival in Port Lyttelton we were put in quarantine. We cast our anchor on the 9th instant and landed the passengers on the 10th by the ship's boats, at the quarantine station. Being both mentally and bodily weak, I applied to Dr. Donald for additional medical assistance, Dr. McLean was sent down to assist. I next applied to be relieved of my duty as surgeon-superintendent in charge of the emigrants; Dr. Donald kindly assented. It is not my wish to speak of matters personal to myself, or to the onerous duty I have had to perform on board the ship, it was almost continuous, day and night. I did not grumble, but, sir, I do now grumble at the stigma attempted to be cast on the character and conduct of those in command of the ship and passengers, &c. I fearlessly challenge the strictest enquiry into my professional and moral conduct during a passage of 138 days, and, indeed, under circumstances the most trying to a medical man at sea it is not alone disease we have to contend against, but the causes of disease, bad air, overcrowding, & c. Throughout the passage I received every assistance from Captain Glendinning whose constant remark to me was, "Doctor, if there is anything in the ship you think the passengers require it is at your service." The passengers and emigrants conducted themselves during the voyage with much order and propriety. I unhesitatingly state it as my opinion that no ship ever entered Port Lyttelton on board of which less immorality existed than on board the *Brother's Pride*. I must apologise, sir, for occupying so much of your space. I beg to thank Dr. Donald for his gentlemanly and courteous conduct to me. I regret to state that it is not in my power to express that opinion of Captain Sproul, pilot and harbour-master, who might with benefit to himself cultivate a less overbearing manner. He it was who, I believe, first raised reports prejudicial to the ship *Brother's Pride* and those in connexion with her, a subject that, perhaps, by and by may require explanation. I am, & c., Fitzherbert Dermott, Surgeon.[38]

John Whitelaw was outraged at Dr Dermott's letter and sent a replying letter to the editor of the *Lyttelton Times*. John was still at the Quarantine Station, Camp Bay and the date of this letter was 4 January 1864. He ended his letter:

"I presently refrain from blowing more holes through this gossamer web of a story, in the hope that sufficient has been stated to show that enquiry is much needed into this melancholy case. Enquiry has been requested by the authorities by five sixths of the married men, joined by several of the unmarried. Dr. Dermott invites it, and with propriety, he *found the* ship overcrowded, at Gravesend, *did not make her so,* and should not be stigmatized for errors not his own. Hoping the authorities will not fail to make a thorough investigation into both outfit and management of our ill-starred ship."[42]

The Voyage of the *Brother's Pride*

Map of the Journey of the *Brother's Pride* 1863

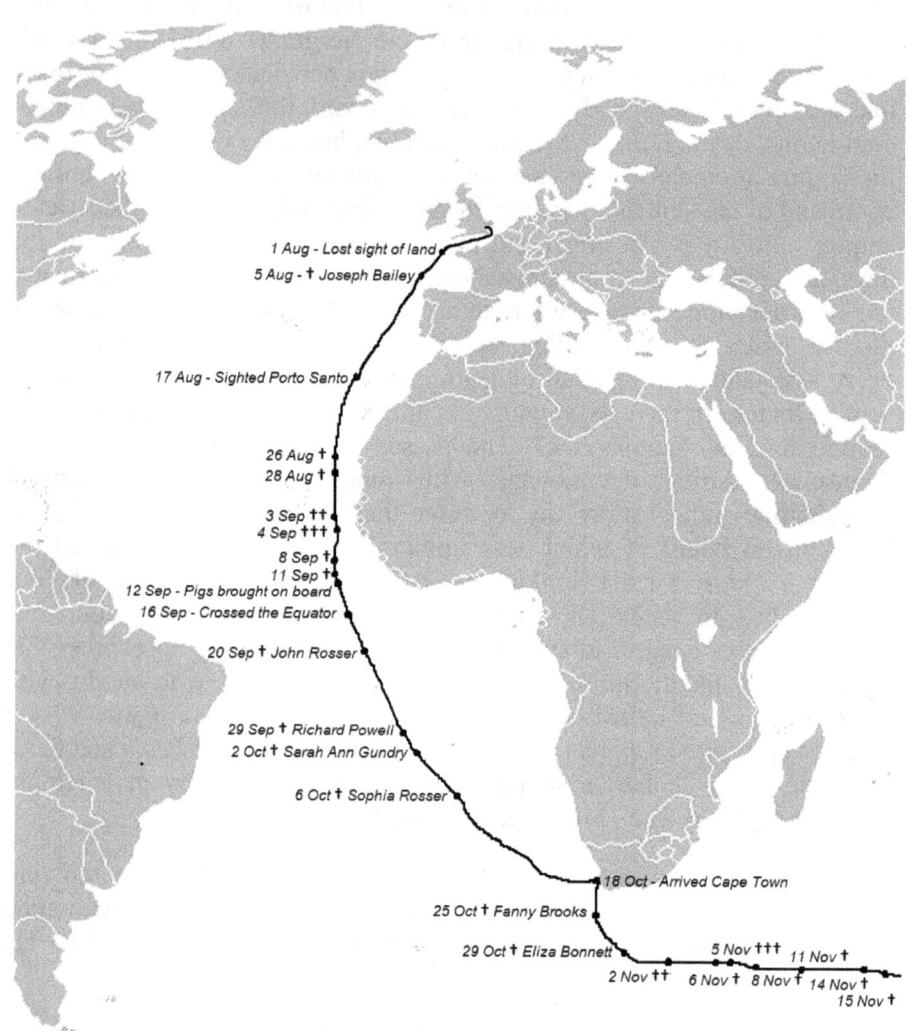

(23 July 1863 – 9 December 1863)

Arrival of Two Ships

In the *Otago Daily Times* on 7 December 1863 it was stated that "The ships *Bahia* and *Brother's Pride* are now out some days longer than the *Pekin*, and are looked for hourly with a change of wind from the S.W." They had received this report from the *Lyttelton Times* and with the delay in reporting didn't realise that the ships had arrived at the heads of Lyttelton that very day. The ships' arrival would have been a relief to family and friends in the colony as the ships had taken so long to arrive. They were seen in the offing (part of the sea visible to a person standing on the shore) on the evening of Sunday 6 December 1863 and arrived at the heads the next day. There was a flagpole at Diamond Harbour on which raised flags were indicating to Lyttelton that two ships could be sighted. These stayed up all Monday. Captain Sproul of the Lyttelton Harbour pilot boat boarded the *Bahia* and enquired after the name of the other ship which he was soon told was *Brother's Pride*. Captain Sproul then boarded the *Brother's Pride* and discovered a ship in a bad state. He was refused charge of the ship to take it into port. Sproul offered to go back to shore and get fresh supplies for the sick children on board, but Captain Glendinning refused this help. Captain Sproul stayed overnight on the ship and returned on the pilot boat the next day with news for those on shore. The *Brother's Pride* had "more than the average amount of sickness" according to one of the newspapers, but the reporters didn't know the full story yet.[48] News from the *Bahia* was that all passengers were well.[49]

Bahia was anchored off the Port Levy Heads and *Brother's Pride* quite a way north of Godley Heads. They were instructed to stay where they were until the SW gales died down and it was easier to sail into Lyttelton Harbour.[49]

On 9 December 1863, the news became clearer to reporters for the *Press* and *Lyttelton Times*. They learnt that the *Brother's Pride* had endured 44 [actually 46] deaths on board and this had created a "great sensation" in port. The Captain had refused the ship to be piloted on Monday and the ship had to be boarded a second time on the Tuesday 8 December to pilot it to Camp Bay in Lyttelton Harbour. The ship was awaiting a medical inspection to determine whether quarantine was warranted or not.[26] They were ordered to hoist the Yellow Jack, the maritime flag to indicate infectious disease on board.

According to H. B. Kirk's account, the *Brother's Pride* and *David G. Fleming* were both trying to make it into Lyttelton Harbour on 8 December and the *David G. Fleming* got in first. Almost at once, the wind whipped around to the south west and the *Brother's Pride* was stuck outside the harbour. The Captain, in frustration, turned the ship north and "swore he would take the ship to South America." This caused the women on board to scream and for many tears to flow. Captain Glendinning let the ship go quite a way north until the passengers could see the windmill which had been removed from Windmill Road in Christchurch (around 1863) and erected at Leithfield. Eventually the Captain calmed down and turned the ship around.[37]

The *Bahia* on the other hand safely anchored at Rhodes Bay (now called Purau Bay) in Lyttelton Harbour on Monday morning, 7 December, at 10am. She was 137 days out![26] Some of the faster boats of the time did the journey in just over 80 days, if they struck favourable weather conditions.

On 9 December the *Brother's Pride* finally entered Lyttelton Harbour.[37] The ship was visited by Immigration Commissioners who found a ship in a very poor state with sick passengers on board. They worked out that typhus, scarlet fever and low fever had been rampant. Many had also died of general debility after having these diseases. The ship was put into quarantine at Camp Bay on 10 December 1863; the total journey being 139 days long, or 4 months and 16 days. However, on the first day of quarantine, Captain Glendinning took it upon himself to flout the law and take the ship into the main harbour area among other ships. He pulled up astern of the *Lancashire Witch*.[50] This was contrary to quarantine regulations and Glendinning was given a stern warning by the Harbourmaster Captain Sproul to return to Camp Bay at the first change of wind.

A tragically long list of 46 deaths was published in the *Press* on 10 December along with 11 births and one marriage.[39]

```
BIRTHS.
04 Aug.   Christina Mackay           a daughter.
12 Aug.   Esther Roberts             a daughter.
03 Sep.   J. Elizabeth McLaughlin    a son.
09 Sep.   Isabella Helm [Helem]      a son.
18 Sep.   Eliza Bonnett              a son.
03 Oct.   M. Hathaway                a son.
20 Oct.   Henrietta Hamilton         a daughter.
25 Oct.   Barbara Stout              a son.
11 Nov.   Hannah Trigg               twins, both males.
14 Nov.   Janet Brown                a son.
```

MARRIAGES
23 Sep.　James Shepherd, 2nd mate, to Jane McWilliam.

DEATHS.
05 Aug.	Joseph Bailey	2 years 9 months.
26 Aug.	W. Scrimshaw	1 year 3 months.
28 Aug.	S. M. Thomas	9 months.
03 Sep.	Margaret McWilliam	4 years
03 Sep.	Wm. Powell,	6 years.
04 Sep.	Eda Powell	2 years
04 Sep.	Tom Webb	3 years
04 Sep.	Isaac Shelton	33 years
08 Sep.	Clara Webb	1 year.
11 Sep.	Mary Cole	8 years.
20 Sep.	John Rosser	(married) 24 years.
29 Sep.	Richard Powell	24 years.
02 Oct.	Sarah Ann Gundy (misspelt Gundry)	(single) 17 years.
06 Oct.	Sophia Rosser	(widow) 22 years.
25 Oct.	Fanny Brooks	44 years.
29 Oct.	Eliza Bonnett	29 years.
02 Nov.	John Ellery	(son of Mrs. Ellery)
02 Nov	John Collett	8 years 6 months.
05 Nov.	Jessie Helem	3 years 6 months
05 Nov.	Samuel Hawkins	8 months
05 Nov	James Edward Birch	11 months.
06 Nov.	son of H. & E. Bonnett	1 year 6 months.
08 Nov.	Edith B. Norbury	4 years.
11 Nov.	Andrew McMillan	13 months.
14 Nov.	Mary E. Brassington	1 year 10 months
14 Nov.	Agnes Brown	2 years 6 months.
15 Nov.	Andrew Crosbie	8 years.
16 Nov.	Robert Brown	7 years.
17 Nov.	Emma Carter	5 years
17 Nov.	Frances Eaton	(single) 28 years.
21 Nov.	Margaret Anderson	(single) 23 years
21 Nov.	John Johnstone	15 months
21 Nov.	Henry Voyce [Voice]	1 year 9 months.
22 Nov.	Janet Brown	29 years
22 Nov.	David Brown	(son of Janet) 5 years.
23 Nov.	George Bonnett	15 months.

24 Nov.	infant son of Janet Brown	2 weeks.
26 Nov.	Thomas Collett	2 years 9 months
27 Nov.	Hannah Trigg	28 years.
29 Nov.	Edward Collett	2 years 9 months.
02 Dec.	Andrew Crosbie	46 years
03 Dec.	Margaret Stout	(single) 35 years.
04 Dec.	Charlotte Williams	40 years.
06 Dec.	Infant son of A. & H. Trigg	No age given
06 Dec.	Benjamin Nicholls (son of H. & E. Nicholls)	No age given
09 Dec.	Cole's son	No age given

The list above adds up to 46 deaths. The newspapers often stated 44 deaths and the passengers' statement says 45 deaths. In any case there were far too many deaths for one immigrant ship voyage, even beating the *Clontarf* which had 41 deaths on arrival in 1860.[17]

People in Christchurch and Lyttelton were fearful of the illness on the *Brother's Pride*. They had endured a bout of scarlet fever brought over on the *Huntress*, which was never quarantined, and were now generally well in the two towns. People didn't want another lot of illness and the word "evil" was used in the paper to describe badly managed emigrant ships. The captain was described as needing punishment for his stupidity in sailing into harbour contrary to regulations. This was probably how most of the local population felt.[51]

Quarantine

On 12 December 1863, it was mentioned in the *Press* that the health of the passengers was improving,[52] and by 22 December the *Lyttelton Times* reported that there had been no fresh case of fever for at least four or five days at Camp Bay.[53] The newspapers failed to report the death of a 2 week old infant named Hathaway on 16 December.[54] The Third Officer had been sent on shore as he was slightly ill, but was perfectly fit to walk the deck.[55] A few days later it was Christmas day and another 6 week old child died, named Trigg.[54] The next day, on 26 December 1863, Dr McLean, the doctor in charge of the quarantined immigrants, reported that the Third Officer was worse, being the most severe case of illness at that time. There were still four patients, with the rest being convalescent. On the same day there was a report that the *Brother's Pride* was admitted to pratique on Thursday morning (24 December 1863) and anchored opposite Lyttelton in the afternoon. Pratique is a licence for a ship to enter port after contagious illness on board.[56] The ship's cargo was being unloaded, but the passengers were still in quarantine until 5 January.[54]

While the passengers were in quarantine in Camp Bay, many started walking away from the quarantine area to explore Banks Peninsula. Some were seen stealing four cases of ale and two cases of whiskey from a delivery which had been made on the shore for Thomas Wood. Thomas saw them at a distance but couldn't make out their faces. The quarantined passengers ran over the hill to get away from him and Thomas was not allowed to enter the quarantine area to find the culprits. He wrote a disgruntled letter to the Editor about keeping the immigrants under control.[57] One of the passengers to leave the quarantine ground was John Whitelaw, who had walked around to Diamond Harbour and found a small hut near the jetty where the passengers had first landed. He had his breakfast at the hut. While there, the owner of the station came down and said hello. He wasn't particularly happy to see a man from quarantine when his wife was extremely scared of the diseases that were on the ship. He also mentioned that he was a Justice of the Peace and that he should arrest John for breaking the quarantine rules.[58]

Before he did any such thing, however, he mentioned that some carpenters he had employed had not arrived from Lyttelton and soon John and the station owner had entered into an agreement. John would sneak out of the quarantine station, without authorities knowing, and complete the carpentry work for him. In return he was given lots of delicious food, including strawberries and cream. He had a great time! The only stipulation was that he wasn't allowed into the farmhouse where the wife was and that his dinner would be served to him in the garden.[58]

There were a few births and deaths while the passengers were at Camp Bay as follows[54]:

BIRTHS
19 Dec.   Mrs James Voice a daughter (Sarah Ann on 18 Dec[59])
27 Dec.   Mrs George Voice of a daughter (Mary Ann[59])
31 Dec.   Mrs Edmonds of a son (Percival Henry on 1 Jan[60])
3 Jan.   Mrs King of a son (Henry on 4 Jan[61])

DEATHS
16 Dec.   An infant named Hathaway   2 months
25 Dec.   An infant named Trigg   6 weeks

When compared to other records the above dates are often one day wrong (see the alternative dates in brackets). Maybe the Doctor was one day out in his diary? Some records (such as newspaper articles on the *Brother's Pride* reunions) claim there were four deaths in the quarantine camp but the other two cannot be proven at this stage. Apparently out of 74 burials at Camp Bay only 20 were ever recorded.

After the quarantine had finished on 5 January[54] the passengers got back on the ship for the Port of Lyttelton. The women and children were taken around to Sumner by sea while the men were left to walk over the hills to Ferrymead where it appears they boarded a small train to meet their families.[58] Dr William McLean and Mr McKay, back at Camp Bay, piled up the immigrant's rubbish and burned it.[54]

On 9 January there was a comment in the papers that the Immigration Commissioners had given a very bad report on the *Brother's Pride* regarding discipline onboard. Some events that happened on board were "unfit for publication," being obviously too vile to print. We never do find out exactly what this is about, although there are some suggestions in the records which are commented on later in this book.

A letter was written by Doctor William McLean regarding the quarantine site at Camp Bay. The long quarantine period of the *Brother's Pride* passengers proved to be a test case for the quarantine site and this showed up quite a few problems that needed to be remedied as follows[54]:

1. The site itself was good.
2. The houses were badly constructed, in that water was leaking in during storms. The zinc tiles on the roof were not nailed down enough, the nails being too short and as Dr McLean puts it, "everything about these houses seems to preach of cheapness."
3. Ventilation was poor in the houses and the Doctor suggested there be a permanent ventilator as the occupants tended to close all the windows and doors up at night and the air in the morning was "poisonous."
4. It would have been easy for water to be supplied by iron pipes for drinking, cooking and the water closet at very little expense.
5. Drains could have been covered with tiles instead of being exposed.
6. The water closets and refuse heaps were too "prominent" whatever this means. Maybe they were far too close to the quarantine huts. In any case one can imagine they smelt very bad.
7. The wash house should have been down by the sea next to the creek, with posts in the ground and washing lines attached.
8. There was no luggage room, which was very much needed.

9. A small lock up would have been useful.
10. The hospital should have been further away from the other houses and surrounded by a wall or fence.
11. The boundary of the quarantine site needed to be more clearly marked. This was probably so that the people didn't roam further than they should.
12. The Superintendent "ought to be active, steady and honest. If he is civil, so much the better." Obviously the superintendent at the time was none of these things!

All in all, the quarantine site at Camp Bay was pretty primitive and life there would have been fairly tough, although a huge relief generally, compared to the confines and horrors of the *Brother's Pride*.

Camp Bay Cemetery

This lovely piece about the Camp Bay Cemetery was written to the Editor of the *Press* in 1916, many years after the first pioneers.

"Sir, — In the suburbs of our fair cities we occasionally leave the highway to visit some, flower-spangled where trim and well-kept paths lead us through a maze of costly headstones. There, the hired gardener may be seen at work upon a blaze of floral beauty before a colossal stone, while nearby a lady, draped in black, removes with loving hand the tiny weed that is an interloper in a natty square of green. But, far from the highways and the byways, in a sunny corner, seldom-visited save by fishermen and shepherds, there is a little graveyard that is not so well attended to. On a low-lying point of land, in the south-east corner of Camp Bay, Lyttelton Harbour, there stood, years ago, the barracks that afforded temporary shelter to those brave pioneers who left their native land and cheerfully faced the elements to seek new homes among the roadless swamps and virgin forests of New Zealand. But, during the long voyages in the small, overcrowded sailing vessels of that time, fever wrought havoc; among the aspiring; colonists. Many died, and were buried at sea, while others lingered until reaching land, when they were reverently laid to rest by relatives or by fellow-passengers, in the little cemetery before the group of barracks at Camp Bay. To-day the fragments of a post-and-rail fence, long since ruthlessly destroyed, encircle the resting place of quite a score of loved ones, to whose gravesides, perhaps, the tender thoughts of mourners in other lands are ever wont to wander. Here and there, upon a piece of rough-hewn sandstone, some letters are still decipherable, but, with the fast-crumbling stone, the name upon it will soon be lost to sight and memory. Tussocks and rushes are Nature's only adornments in the little cemetery, and sheep graze at will upon the graves. Wool may be a valuable product, but it stands to the everlasting discredit of the people of Canterbury to be raising it from the graves of the early pioneers. Those straight rows of little mounds on the low spur above Camp Bay tell all too clearly of the price paid by our forefathers for our beautiful and fertile country. Surely a spot so sacred and historical is worthy of better keeping. Three chains of fencing across the narrow neck of land, the grubbing of the rushes, and the planting of a few shrubs in the unused area of the enclosure, would be a start towards the fulfilment of our provincial duty, and would do much to secure, to beautify, and to indicate this desolate burial ground. —Yours, etc. Oliver Hunter. Church Bay, February 14th."

The Queen Vs Captain Glendinning

Captain Glendinning was put to trial after his misconduct at the Port of Lyttelton. On 19 January 1864 Captain Glendinning was charged with refusing and neglecting to take a pilot on board on the evening of 6 December. The Doctor, Captain and Sproul testified over what had happened on board the day the *Brother's Pride* arrived.[62]

Captain Sproul was the pilot on that night. He claimed he boarded the vessel at about 10pm to take charge as he usually did, before piloting the ship into the harbour. He asked questions regarding the health of the passengers and crew and asked them to give 15 more fathoms of chain and to point the yards to the wind. Captain Sproul said he was introduced to the Captain by the Doctor. Captain Glendinning said he didn't require a pilot and went on deck. When Captain Sproul got there, all his orders had been countermanded. Sproul asked for two lights to be hoisted so his pilot boat would know to come back for him, but Glendinning refused, so Sproul stayed the night on deck. After much trouble getting the ensign hoisted to recall his boat the next morning, it was finally done. Sproul boarded his boat and went to the *Bahia*.

While on board the previous day, Sproul had asked the Doctor about the sickness and deaths on board and the Doctor mentioned they needed provisions such as wine for the ill passengers. Sproul said "My dear man, or my dear sir, if you had required anything I would have sent my boat to fetch it." This angered the Doctor as he was not used to being spoken to in an informal colonial manner, only addressed as a gentleman. "My dear man," upset him. Also the Doctor claimed Sproul called the ship "dirty" and commented that they had experienced a great many deaths. Obviously, this was offensive to the doctor.

Captain Glendinning was just outside the door and heard the Doctor and someone else (Sproul) using "unpleasant words" about sickness and deaths, spoken in an "angry way." He claimed Sproul never introduced himself as the pilot and Harbourmaster and this was backed up by Doctor Dermott and Chief Officer, Mr Jameson, who both thought he was a stranger from the shore. The Captain said Sproul took no notice of him in the cabin, so he went back on deck. The Chief Officer didn't think Sproul was a pilot saying: "I looked on Captain Sproul as a loafer going about in a boat giving orders." Loud laughter was heard from the court at this remark![63]

Because the crew claimed they didn't know who Sproul was and the regulations were somehow mislaid and not viewed (even though Sproul claimed they were laid on a table, on that first boarding), the court dismissed the charge.[62]

What version of events were true, we will never know. Maybe Captain Sproul was an overbearing kind of character, but it seems also that Captain Glendinning was at the very least a little bit scatter brained, if not an outright liar about the events of that night. From accounts given he seemed to be a stubborn man who didn't like being given orders by anyone and often couldn't control his crew.

Another Court Case

Alexander Rose who was Landing Surveyor of Her Majesty's Customs, Lyttelton and also Immigration Officer gave a statement regarding Captain Glendinning breaching clauses 157 and 159 of the Merchant Shipping Act, 1854, for "shipping seamen contrary to the provisions of the said act."

Captain Glendinning gained 16 passengers at Cape Town, only one of which paid for his passage to New Zealand. Glendinning took the men on as seamen but five or six of them were "odd men" and only nine were able seamen. They were unable to pay, and therefore worked for their passage out.

Captain Glendinning was very unsure about whom exactly the sixteen men were when Alex Rose asked for a list of names. Rose later told Captain Glendinning that he had "taken proceedings against him for breach of the law." Glendinning couldn't understand why!

Glendinning then changed his story, saying the men were stowaways who wanted to get to New Zealand. On arrival he didn't hand in their names as passengers, and did not report them or write them down in his log, except for three, who Glendinning admitted to shipping. Glendinning stated he didn't know the stowaways were on board until after they had left the Cape, especially since he had 400 or 500 people on board. He told the stowaways that they must find their own provisions.

One of the stowaways Thomas Maloney gave a statement:

"I went on board the *Brother's Pride* at the Cape of Good Hope. I got a waterman to put me alongside. I am a seaman, and went on board, and stowed away in the ship the night I got on board. About two or three days after we got to sea, I saw the Captain. He mustered myself and a number of others on the poop. We were mustered to see who were stow-aways. There seemed to be 15 to 20. I was a stow-away as well as the rest. He said to the mate "here's a fine lot of stow-aways." He took my name down. He said, "you will have plenty of work and nothing to eat." I did work as a seaman on board. I was in watch; sometimes captain of the main-deck. It was my duty to see the passengers kept themselves clean. I was working as a seaman and in other capacities till we got to the Quarantine Ground. The Captain took my name when we were mustered. I don't remember that he asked me to sign articles. I am very forgetful at times. I have been moonstruck." [45] There was laughter from the court at this statement![64]

Thomas was given no provisions on board. He was dressed like an immigrant and mixed with the passengers and had "just come down the country and was starving."[45]

Richard Rae also got on board from a waterman's boat. He saw the Captain only on the third day as well and was worked hard with no provisions.[45]

Captain Glendinning was liable under the Act for taking on the stowaway seamen as workers without entering into an agreement with them. In his defence Glendinning stated that it was several days before he realised he had stowaways and that it was impossible to distinguish them among 400 or 500 people on board. He also complained that "such an outcry should be made about his ship," and thought it very wrong for people to act towards him with such vindictive feeling. The Bench obviously took pity on him as they decided to dismiss the case with costs.[64]

Some of the public were extremely upset at Glendinning getting away without punishment. One member of the public, named "Observer," quoted an almost identical case in Australia where the captain of the *King of the Seas* was charged large fines, or to be sentenced to 3 months in prison. This ship gained 26 stowaways from the Cape and the Captain never reported them. "Observer" also stated that the stowaways on board the *Brother's Pride* had to rely on begging for food from the passengers and crew who only just got enough food for themselves.

The extra stowaways were just another unnecessary burden on the poor passengers who were on an already tragic ship!

The *Brother's Pride* Enquiry

The passengers on the *Brother's Pride* wrote a petition to the Provincial Government regarding their ill-fated journey. The passengers wrote the petition on 7 December 1863 while still on board the *Brother's Pride*.[65] They stated there were 45 deaths during the journey (actually 46). They quoted the Passenger's Act that was put in place in 1855, obviously getting advice from someone in regards to their rights. Alex Rose, the Immigration Officer based in Lyttelton, sent a copy of the petition on to the Provincial Government in order to gain authority to proceed with the enquiry. John Whitelaw seemed to be the leader of the petition. His signature was at the top of the list of passenger names[65] and he had the first statement, before anyone else. He also wrote a scathing letter to the editor while trapped in quarantine at Camp Bay.[42]

After reading the passengers' complaints, the Provincial Government decided to proceed with the enquiry against the Master of the ship, plus chief crew.[65] The enquiry into the *Brother's Pride* tragedy was undertaken mainly due to the "excessive mortality"[65] experienced by the passengers on the ship but also because of other unsuitable ship arrangements.

The 9 main points of the petition were as follows:[65]

1. **Lack of Space**
   The married couples' compartment gave 16 square feet of space only, instead of the 18 square feet recommended by the Passenger's Act. Because of the arrangement of things in this compartment some areas of the ship gave only 13 feet 6 inches of space. There were 268 human beings crammed into this compartment. Far too many!
2. **Medical Examination at Gravesend**
   The medical examination was a farce, with the passengers only having to answer to their names when called out and point out their children. There was no actual medical examination before boarding to determine if sickness was being brought on board.

3. **Cooking Arrangements**
   The passengers had no experienced or competent cook appointed before leaving and one was eventually found after three weeks at sea.
4. **Filthy and Insufficient Decks**
   The decks from the Tropics onwards had 7 dogs, 9 pigs and 5 sheep running around loose and defecating into the water already on the deck surface. This made the area filthy and stinking. The men walking on the deck found this area overcrowded (with animals and humans) and disgusting. This deck water was dropping through cracks in the non-watertight deck and making bedding wet for several passengers for days and weeks at a time. Further enquiry into these accusations showed the ship decks were cleaned and scraped about twice a week, but that the dogs had been smuggled on after the Commissioners had been on board to check conditions at Gravesend. Five of the dogs belonged to Mr James Johnston and they were washed down every day. From further statements it appears the so called loose animals were sometimes let out, but not all the time.
5. **Bad Water in the Tropics**
   Unboiled or "nauseous" water was given to passengers in the Tropics.
6. **The Stop at Cape of Good Hope**
   When medical supplies were bought at the Cape they were not anywhere near on the scale needed for the amount of sickness on board. The passengers considered the sickness an "emergency" and that supplies of a much larger scale should have been bought.
7. **Delayed Voyage and Supplies Running Out**
   If the stop at the Cape was not needed then it was a very bad decision indeed. It delayed the whole journey by three weeks which meant that food for invalids, such as sago, arrowroot, wine, brandy and preserved milk ran out. The passengers considered that the 17 deaths in the last 21 days were in part due to the invalid dietary supplies running out. However quite a few statements at the actual enquiry said there were plenty of provisions handed out and that their children had been given the necessary medicines.
8. **Lack of Inspections**
   There were no regular inspections in regards to cleanliness of berths or persons on board; "the filthy finding too much liberty to revel in their filth." It appears that the passengers should have been mustered every Sunday, but this was not done. Bedding was only aired occasionally when weather permitted.

9. **The Hospital**
It was situated in the lower deck which was not suitable. It was in the worst and most uncomfortable part of the lower deck. The passengers thought a "very unexperienced individual was selected," possibly meaning Doctor Dermott. Several passengers commented that Doctor Dermott was drunk or simply refused to attend to the sick. Sometimes he said that children were fine until only a few minutes before dying. In that time, no invalid foods or medicines were given to them. There appeared to be a few drunken nights in question. One was when he fell into the bed where Mrs Mason was lying. The Doctor claims vehemently that he was not worse for drink although he claims he did drink freely while on board, due to the stress. The Doctor's surgery was on the upper deck and had medical supplies in it. The Doctor claimed he slept in there as the supplies were being stolen. At one stage a man did touch the brandy cask and brandy was running down into the 'tween decks. So the room was not used as a surgery and everyone was crammed into one small hospital when there should have been two, separating the men from women and children.

Alex Rose wrote a letter on 9 January 1864 which listed which parts of the Passenger Act had been breached. They were as follows:[41]

1. **Hospital**
There was an infringement of Clause 24. in not using the hospital on deck and instead keeping it as a storeroom and bedroom for the Doctor. The one that was used was "crammed indiscriminately with men, women and children."
2. **Cooking Arrangements**
Clause 39 had been infringed by there not being a qualified cook on board and the fact the Master admitted he knew about this.
3. **Animals on Board**
The ship had pigs and one dog over the specified allowance in Clause 8, Section 6. Pigs were not allowed on ships as provisions if they were not kept clean or were of "annoyance to passengers."

The fact the passengers had been "assaulted" and money extorted from them when crossing the line was not covered by the Passenger Act, but the Provincial Government could "cause them to be reimbursed, and take the most severe measures against the Captain and owner, or agents." The fact the Master and Surgeon had knowledge of the extortion meant they had more grounds to prosecute. Alex Rose did not intend to prosecute unless the Provincial Government wanted to go ahead. He said they could withhold the gratuities and also the balance unpaid of passage money, due to the brokers in London, so it wouldn't happen again in the future.[41]

The Provincial Government obviously decided to go ahead as evidence for this case was taken on 15 January 1864 before the Executive Council at the Government Buildings.

The statements of the passengers were interesting as they often contradicted each other, adding confusion to the petition. They also gave a background story to the journey. They are written in full in the Appendix and go into detail about individual passengers and their plights.

Gratuities Withheld

The Provincial Council was to pay gratuities to the head crew of the *Brother's Pride* but, due to the enquiry, it was decided that the gratuities would probably be withheld and the Captain and crew would have to go back to England with their tales between their legs, unless they could prove that they were not at fault in the mismanagement of the ship. Whether or not they were actually withheld is not stated in the records.

The gratuities in a letter dated 23 October (i.e. before the ship arrived) were as follows[66]:

Captain	£25
Surgeon	50 Guineas
Chief Officer	£10
Officer in charge of dishing out provisions	£5
One or two nurses	£2 to £5 each

The Sale of Passenger Effects

The problem with people dying on long sea journeys is what to do with the trunk and items left on the docks at Lyttelton after unloading. Some passengers had no family to send effects to, or sometimes it was just not worth the effort. One such case was Isaac Shelton, who died on the *Brother's Pride* on 4 September 1863. The sale of his effects raised the measly amount of £2 12s. It appears the proceeds probably went to the Provincial Council.[67]

A Letter from Fitzherbert Dermott

Dr Dermott had probably suffered from a group of accusing passengers and an angry public at the *Brother's Pride* enquiry. He wanted to leave in case he spoke ill of those in charge of the *Brother's Pride*, as he must have thought the whole voyage badly managed. He wrote a letter to inform the Provincial Government of his intentions of leaving Canterbury.[68]

1 February 1864

The Honbl

    The Provincial Secretary

Sir

I respectfully request that you will cause to be forwarded for me to the care of Messrs Peacock & Co. at Lyttelton a copy of the minutes of the Executive Council in the recent investigation respecting the Officers of the Ship "Brothers Pride"

I purpose leaving for Melbourne this day and lest hereafter my unpleasant allusions be made regarding those who were in authority during the Voyage of the Brother's Pride. I earnestly request your compliance with my application.

I have the honor to be, Sir

Your obliged & faithful

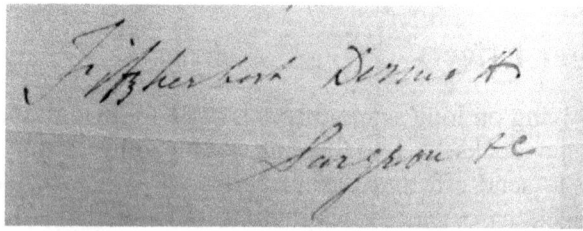

What happened to Fitzherbert Dermott? He eventually came back to New Zealand. He appears in 1872 as the surgeon to the Sea View Lunatic Asylum in Hokitika.[69] Sadly in 1879, Fitzherbert Dermott, Esq., M.R.C.S. London, the sixth son of William Dermott, Esq., of Nappa House, County Cavan, Ireland, died at the young age of 46. He was residing in Revell Street, Hokitika at the time of his death.[70] His mother, who also lived in New Zealand, relied on him for support and was left destitute.[71]

Immorality on Board the *Brother's Pride*

An article in the *Lyttelton Times,* dated 9 January 1864, stated that the Immigration Commissioner's report was divided into two parts, one that was "understood to be unfit for publication." Apparently, it contained "disgraceful conduct" which had taken part on board the ship.[72] Exactly what happened we may never know but there are some suggestions that some "abandoned women" were on board.

Jane F. Mewes [Mewse] was listed as being an 18-year-old domestic servant from Surrey, situated in the single women's compartment.

After arrival, Jane was living at Mr E. S. Dalgetty's place. On 4 January 1865, the Provincial Council contacted her for payment of the 7 pounds she owed them for the passage out. Jane refused to pay the money on "plea of minority" at the date of signing the contract, aged only sixteen. The contract was signed outside of New Zealand and therefore she did not consider herself responsible.[73]

The writer of the letter to the Provincial Council, Richard Armstrong, noted, "This girl was on the "Town" for some time after her arrival, and I very much doubt whether her character in her present situation would bear strict inquiry."

Richard was politely stating that Jane was a prostitute of bad character and dubious morals, currently living in sin.

A note scrawled on the corner of the document states, "It will be better to let cases of this kind quietly drop. The claim cannot be legally enforced and considerable care and discretion are necessary in attempting to obtain payment from single women."

Jane's letter is as follows:[73]

"11-1-65

Mr J. Edwin March

Immigration Office

Sir,

The Provincial Government agent having taken my Promissory Note knowing at the same time I was not of age, therefore not responsible, also the contract not having been signed in New Zealand I have no intention of paying any further amount. You may take any legal proceedings where the question as to my liability will be argued by my solicitor in the mean time.

I remain Sir

Yours &

(Signed) Jane Frances Mewes

P.S. This is in answer to yours dated 4th Jan^y /65. With regard to my age I refer you to passengers list at Custom House "Brother's Pride"

Jane wasn't the only immoral person on board the *Brother's Pride*. There was another woman who was named in a list of prostitutes from 1867 as Elizabeth Smith.[74] She doesn't appear in the passenger list, only a Christina Smith. Often prostitutes went by aliases so she may have been a completely different name on the passenger list. Whether she practiced any immorality on board the *Brother's Pride* is unknown. The matron did state that the single girls were well behaved on board but were hard to control in the quarantine camp.[75]

As for the married women, Elizabeth Powell (incorrectly named as Mrs Powers) was accused of sleeping with single man George Richards (incorrectly named Richardson), in the hospital while she was acting as nurse to the patients. Elizabeth lost her husband Richard and two year old girl Eda (Ida) and was understandably devastated by her loss. She was in a terribly sad situation.[75] Some passengers had accused them of sleeping in the same bed, but others who were often in the hospital swore that she never slept with him, only her sister.[75] Whatever the case was, people were probably trying to protect them. They married soon after arriving in New Zealand and they had at least four children in New Zealand.[28] This suggests that maybe something *was* going on between them during the voyage!

Still Notorious Five Years Later

The *Timaru Herald* published an article five years after the arrival of the *Brother's Pride* that suggested the notoriousness of the *Brother's Pride* journey had not been forgotten by the public five years later. However it wasn't the high death count that was mentioned, but the "abandoned women" on board. The enquiry into the journey, however, seems to squash all accusations of abandoned women, especially the matron's statement. Maybe the public knew more than was ever written in the records. This article is interesting, as it shows what some people thought about immigration in the 1860s in Canterbury and how "evil" it was.

"IMMIGRATION. From the *Timaru Herald*, Aug. 29[1868]

If there is one public duty more than another in which the Provincial Government of Canterbury has singly failed, it is in immigration. We say this advisedly, for abundant proof is every day at hand to bear out the assertion that our immigration has been a failure — an expensive, gigantic failure, and the evils of which there is no remedying. From first to last the system under which immigration has been for years carried on in Canterbury has been a bad one, and one calculated rather to produce evil than good to the country to which it has been applied. The gentlemen who from time to time have represented the interests of the province in England, although perhaps desirous of doing their utmost in forwarding those interests, have undoubtedly been most unsuccessful in the matter of immigration; and whether that non-success is owing to personal ignorance as to the best means to be adopted for carrying on a beneficial immigration or whether they were the victims of a system which, by long precedent, they were bound to follow, we will not now enquire. Sufficient for the present purpose is it to say, that for years past the immigration from England to this province, instead of being an absolute boon to this country, as it should have been, has in too many instances proved to be a curse.

We hold that in establishing an immigration agency in England, the locale for an office is not by any means a first consideration, and that if immigration is to be of any practical value, its success should be due entirely to individual work on the part of the immigration agent, and not rely on any such adventitious aid as may accrue from an office being situated in the most business or most fashionable part of a town. But the provincial authorities have thought otherwise, and to all appearance have imagined that the selection of offices in about, the most expensive part of London was necessary to secure the object sought for. Offices in Charing Cross are very expensive to occupy; but we maintain that offices in that quarter of London, putting aside their expensiveness, were wholly unnecessary, and did not promote the cause of immigration one iota, if not actually damaging to it. London is not the place to pick up the class of people required for the colonies. In London you do not find the true agricultural labourer, or do you, as a rule, find the best class of female domestic servants. These two classes should furnish the greatest bulk of our immigrants, and let us ask, have the majority of people sent out in the last few years been of these classes? We unhesitatingly say they have not been. And what have they been? In very many instances immigrants sent to Canterbury have been from a class from which spring the idlers and the good-for-nothings of a town, and on several occasions single women have been sent whose antecedents did not bear investigation, and whose scandalous behaviour, both on board ship and after being landed, pointed them to be of a class better out of a country than in it. Still, these wretched women were doubtless shipped as domestic servants, and the province has to pay the same for them as if they had been of that useful class, of which a few here are to be found. It seems to us that anyone who applies to the agent in London is shipped for Canterbury without the slightest enquiry as to previous character, and without the slightest investigation as to the applicant's adaptability to the requirements of the colony. In proof of this, witness the shipment of numbers of abandoned women in the ship *Brothers' Pride*, which arrived in 1863. The shipment by this vessel we mention as being the most notorious and scandalous of any either before or after that year, but there has hardly been a vessel arriving in Lyttelton with single women that has not been largely tainted with those of the worst description. Do not we repeatedly see in the Christchurch papers' sad proof of this assertion? In the *Press* of last Tuesday is one to hand. The case was one of an "unfortunate" who was found dead on the footpath, with a bottle of brandy by her side, a late arrival by the Gainsborough. Witness also the case of Esther Hoskin, who created quite a sensation in Christchurch some few months since by confessing to having committed a murder in England, just previous to coming to the province. In her case, not the least enquiry as to previous character could have been made by the agent, for we find in an English newspaper of a late date the following paragraph :—"Esther Hoskin, whose circumstantial confession, at New Zealand, of murdering her sweetheart by stabbing him and throwing him over a cliff near Helston, has been reported in this paper, was two years indicted at Bodmin assizes for arson, and acquitted on the ground of insanity. The man she says she murdered is alive in California."

We think there is abundant evidence to prove generally the worthlessness of the immigrants shipped from England to Canterbury, a large number of both men and women having been sent who are not only worthless as colonists, but their presence in the country has been conducive to positive harm. It is only fair however, to say that we do not include all immigrants in our condemnation, for domestic servants of good character and really proficient in every respect have been brought out in ships with the most worthless of their sex. How can we, in the face of this, expect others of good character to come to New Zealand, when it is known that they are liable to be mixed up with those who are not fit company for them? Space does permit us at present to enter further into this question, but we purpose doing so on a future occasion.[76]

Hope for the Future

Many of those on board the *Brother's Pride* who lost loved ones went on to make a decent life for themselves, often remarrying or having more children. I guess they had no other choice but to move on and make the best of what they had. A check of the parish records in the Christchurch City Libraries[77] reveals a lot. The following are some examples:

Henry Williams lost his wife Charlotte on the journey out to New Zealand. He married fellow passenger Elizabeth Ann Benfield (widow) on 21 February 1864 at St Paul's, Papanui, Christchurch. Elizabeth would have been able to look after his 5 children, including William who was an infant.

The witnesses to the above marriage were George Richards and Elizabeth Powell who made their mark (an X) on the parish record. They also met on the journey and married after arrival in New Zealand.

Agnes Crosbie, who lost her 8-year-old son Andrew and her husband Andrew, never remarried and lived to be 82. She was buried with her daughter Jane Blackwood Crosbie in the same grave in Linwood Cemetery. Jane also lived to 82![78]

The Collett family, who suffered great loss with the death of twins Thomas and Edward aged 2 and older brother John aged 8, had a new baby in Christchurch who they named John, born on 28 March 1864. John Collett, father, was a joiner, residing in Addington.

The Bonnett family lost their mother and a child, leaving only three members (a father and two children) after arriving on the *Brother's Pride*. Widowed father Henry Bonnett married Maria Page on 27 April 1867 and had at least one more son. Henry passed away aged 83 in 1913 and was living in the Hillmorton/Spreydon area of Christchurch. His daughter Jane, who survived the journey out, aged 4 years, went on to grow up and marry Samuel Wilson, a carrier, aged 21, on 5 March 1880 at The Manse, Christchurch.

Absalom Trigg lost his wife Anna (Hannah) and twins who were born on the ship (one died on the ship and one in quarantine). He tragically left the quarantine camp alone. He went on to marry Annie Gundy in 1867. There was an Annie Gundy listed in the passenger list as only 13 in 1863 so if this was the same person, Absalom had to wait until she was of legal age before he could marry her.

William Brooks, who lost his wife Ann (Fanny) on the voyage, and was left with two children aged 7 and 4, remarried in 1865 to Anna Downey who was 43, seven years older than him. He was working as a stonemason.

And as for John Brown and his poor wee daughter Margaret Brown aged five; no trace can be found of them. They lost five members of the family on the journey out, including mother Janet. What happened to them we can only guess at, but hopefully John remarried, and Margaret grew up to be healthy and happy.

The Poor Orphan Boy

Charles Rosser was listed as an infant on board the *Brother's Pride*, or 12 to 18 months old according to one account.[37] Tragically his parents John and Sophia both died on board. Charles childhood is unknown but he was possibly looked after by friends in the colony, or the church, or sent to the Christchurch Orphan Asylum, which was open before May 1864.[79] The Asylum was apparently a dirty sort of place and probably not the best start in life, but if he was sent there, at least he was given a chance at life. Charles appears in the records later on in life. He married Mary Ann Perks in 1899. Charles parents were listed as John Charles Rosser and Sophia née Brindle of Gloucestershire. Charles was a labourer living in Linwood, Christchurch. The couple were both 37 and it appears they never had children. Mary Ann was listed as "supposed widow," her husband having not been heard of for 19 years.[77] Charles died in 1942 aged 80 years old and is buried in Linwood Cemetery.[78] It is a relief to see that an orphan managed to survive in a strange land by himself and have a long life. His parents may have unknowingly given him opportunities that he would never have had back in the United Kingdom.

Departures

The *Bahia* left the Port of Lyttelton on 22 January 1864 with Captain Le Fanu still commanding. The ship sailed for Hong Kong, in ballast with no passengers on board.[80] Meanwhile the *Brother's Pride* was still discharging cargo. It was another month before *Brother's Pride* could be cleared for Callao and the ship finally departed on 29 February 1864 with Captain Glendinning still at the helm. There were no passengers on board the *Brother's Pride* thank goodness! This trip to Callao would have been to pick up a load of guano, otherwise known as bird droppings. This would have been a safe cargo for this captain as there was not much he could do to harm it!

Brother's Pride Cargo 1863

There was an article about a screw pile jetty which was arriving on the *Brother's Pride*. An unnamed individual had ordered enough screw piles to make eighty feet of jetty, therefore increasing the jetty accommodation in early 1864, six months earlier than first thought. The piles were purchased by Messrs. Peacock & Co.[81]

There were a few items imported on the ship which were listed in the *Lyttelton Times*. The cargo seems less than average, which probably allowed for more passengers.

> In the Brother's Pride, Peacock and Co., Agents: 95 cases merchandise, 20 casks plaster paris, 2 barrels pitch, Millton and Co.; 4 qr casks spirits, 50 cases, 125 tons coals, 17 cases, 70 casks, 100 casks, 18 casks coals, 10 tons coke, 10 tons pig iron, 200 cases cider, (order) 1 case — Chamier, Esq.; 40 hhds, 100 casks, 10 cases sauces, J, D. Macpherson; 1 case, Richardson; 200 casks, 30 barls. currants, Dalgety and Co.; 5 cases, Morrison and Co,; 1 case, Ward and Reeves; 1 case, Marshall; 20 cast iron screws, 20 do. caps, 20 pile shafts, 20 bracing bars, 1 cask, Wright; 1 case, Harpward; 4 traces, 10 cases, 32,000 fire bricks, 20 hhds. D. Davis; 2 bdls. 1 case, 20 tons coal, White & Co; 1 case, Eskett; 1 do, Harvey; 1 do, Stewart; 2 do, Merton; 3 do, Tucker; 1 box, Webb; 2 kegs, W.W.C.; 1 cask, 3 cases, J. Hall; 1 case, Ellice; 1 cask, Porter; 40 barls, 50 tons coals, Lance; 30 boxes, Thompson and Baldwin; 65 casks, 120 do, soda, 100 casks bottled beer, 50 hhds beer, 108 water casks, 64 tanks, Peacock and Co.

List of Cargo on the Brother's Pride, Lyttelton Times 29 December 1863

Out of Great Tragedy Came Comradeship

Even though the *Brother's Pride* had a lot of tragedy, the passengers still wanted to meet up after 30 years. In a way, the tragedy probably brought them together. The fact they were all confined together for an extra long period of time on board the ship and in quarantine at Camp Bay would have helped friendships develop. There were also many people from the same areas that travelled together, notably the Forest of Dean in Gloucestershire.

Former passenger H. B. Kirk wrote a letter to the editor of the *Star* in 1893, which showed how the passengers had banded together.

"During that long voyage connections were made and acquaintances formed which cannot be severed or forgotten in this life. One marriage, one sale of a wife, eleven births and forty-six deaths (and I believe four others in Camp Bay) made an unenviable record. Let us hope it will never be broken. Now our reunion on Dec. 14 (Thursday next) will be like a meeting of soldiers who fought a battle together thirty years ago, to celebrate their victory. — I am, &c, H. B. KIRK."[37]

This 30 year reunion on 14 December 1893, was the first to be advertised in the newspapers. It was a journey to Diamond Harbour on the *S.S. John Anderson*, with 250 tickets to be distributed.[82] The old shipmates enjoyed themselves at the Diamond Harbour accommodation house. Mrs W. Baker, aged 81, thanked everyone for such a good turnout, and Mr Whitelaw spoke and thanked Messrs Kirk and Hanson who had organised the day. He voted that another reunion should be held and Mr Samuel Bayliss seconded the motion. He said that he was sure they were now all very glad they had come to the colony. Robert Anderson pitched his tent near where the John Anderson, of Charteris Bay, had landed and had lived there ever since, to which he had great applause from the shipmates. Mr Hanson hoped that the misfortunes of the journey 30 years previous would not affect their pleasure that day.[83]

Not surprisingly, some passengers had never been back to Lyttelton Harbour since they arrived in New Zealand.[58]

Some of the passengers went to visit Camp Bay, where they first landed. The old huts had been removed, except for portions of an old one, and then there was the graveyard that held those who died in quarantine.[83] It was noted that four passengers died and were buried there, but the records show only two.[58]

They spent a lovely afternoon at Diamond Harbour,[83] and returned to Lyttelton at about 6pm.[58]

The next reunion was the 32nd reunion, held in 1895 at the grounds of Mr W. Thompson near New Brighton.[84]

The 40th anniversary was on 10 December 1903 and was held at the Colonists Hall in Lyttelton at 10.30 am, with shipmates and their friends being invited. Tickets were available from members of the committee.[85]

The last reunion that can be found was a luncheon that took place on 10

December 1913, which would have been the 50th anniversary of the ship arriving in the Port of Lyttelton. Around 40 shipmates attended, as well as spouses and descendents. Mr H. B. Kirk presided over the event.[86]

Many of the passengers who were adults on the voyage out were starting to die and obituaries were appearing in the newspapers. So this was the end of the reunions.

Passengers on the Brother's Pride

Passengers on the *Brother's Pride*

Anderson

Robert Anderson was born in the Shetland Islands in 1856 and came out with his father William Anderson in 1863 on the *Brother's Pride* aged about 7 years old. Robert Anderson was of Charteris Bay,[58] where his family first farmed after landing in New Zealand. Robert was a member of the Port Victoria Road Board for sixteen years and chairman for quite a few years as well. He was involved in the formation of the Mount Herbert County Council and was chairman for two years. He was also on the Lyttelton Harbour Board. Robert married a daughter of Rev R. R. Bradley and when he died he left two sons and a daughter. He was "of a quiet, unassuming, and kindly nature," and was much respected in the community. Robert Anderson died of pneumonia in 1907 and flags were flown half mast on the Lyttelton Harbour Board offices and other buildings in Lyttelton, as a mark of respect.[87]

Bailey

Samuel Bailey was born in 1829 in Gloucestershire, England. He travelled with his wife and six children to New Zealand on the *Brother's Pride*. His first venture in New Zealand was a blacksmith's shop in Templeton where he did good business for many years. He bought land in the Templeton area and called it Barton Farm, farming as well as doing blacksmith work. He eventually just concentrated on farming, giving up the blacksmith business. Samuel imported three threshing machines and later bought a combine and did very well from them. Samuel was a member of the Templeton school committee for thirty years, twenty-five of those as chairman. He was also on the Templeton Road Board for twenty-eight years. He was one of the directors of the New Zealand Farmers' Co-operative Association from its inception. He was also in the New Zealand Farmers' Fire and Marine Association. In 1901 Samuel and his wife celebrated their golden wedding and at the time had eight sons and one daughter, forty-one grandchildren and two great-grandchildren.[88]

Mr S. Bailey

Bayliss

John Bayliss arrived from Gloucestershire on the ship *Brother's Pride* in 1863 and settled at Mandeville, Canterbury with his parents. He moved to Auckland in about 1883. He married Emma Lofting on 20 December 1883. They had six children and twelve grandchildren alive at the time of their diamond wedding in 1943. They were living in Epsom, Auckland at the time.[89]

Brassington

William Brassington was born about 1837–41 in Nottingham, England and trained to be a stonemason like his father. He travelled to New Zealand on the *Brother's Pride* with his wife Ellen and two daughters. His younger child died on the voyage. He set up business carving stones at a Christchurch Cemetery. His work was of high quality and Provincial Architect Benjamin Mountfort employed him to carve the stonework on the provincial council chamber. William carved flora and fauna indigenous to the province of Canterbury as well as a statues depicting Queen Victoria, her consort and other statesmen as well as popular heroes of the day. There was a rumour that he depicted himself and his favourite barmaid! William was then sought after for his work. He carved the pulpit at the church of St John the Baptist in Latimer Square in 1866, the font at Flaxton Church in 1867 and was commissioned to work on the Christchurch Cathedral. When the cathedral project ran out of money he did building work as a source of income and worked on Lyttelton Harbour and projects at Teddington and Allendale. One of this buildings was the Church of The Holy Innocents in Christchurch, which was finished in 1869. He again worked with Mountfort on the Canterbury Museum in the 1870s and also built the great portico in 1876. William Brassington also worked in partnership with John Kennington to build the castle-like Lyttelton Timeball Station, which was completed in 1876. In 1889 he emigrated to Melbourne, Australia and seemed to be chasing gold. He died in 1905 and was buried in Footcray cemetery, Australia.[90]

Brooks

William Brooks is in an advertisement in the newspapers in 1902 for "Dr William's Pink Pills for pale people." From the advertisements it says that William Brooks was born in Cheshire and emigrated on the *Brother's Pride* on a "long and somewhat monotonous voyage". He was engaged in agricultural pursuits for many years and often worked in swampy land. He used to be fit and hearty but in about 1898 he was gardening and was seized with sciatica. He was cured by Dr William's pink pills for pale people and was sleeping more soundly that he had done for years. It says he lives in Talbot Street, Geraldine, South Canterbury.[6]

Burnett

Alexander Burnett was born in Banffshire, Scotland and travelled to New Zealand on the *Brother's Pride* in 1863. He had a farm section at Temuka for some years before moving to Wairarapa in the North Island. He established sawmills at Taueru and Akura and was also the licensee of the Taueru Hotel. A massive court case connected with his sawmills saw the Privy Council decision going against Mr Burnett. He gave up sawmilling and returned to farming at Fernridge, then in his older years lived permanently in Masterton. He died in 1906, aged sixty three, of consumption which he had for three years, his wife dying twelve years before him. He had two grown up daughters at the time of his death.[91]

Collett

John Collett was born in 1827 in Dudley, West Midlands, England. He was a carpenter and joiner. He married Susan Smith at Stourbridge in 1851 and had six children within eleven years. They travelled on the *Brother's Pride* to New Zealand in 1863. They had tragedy in the family with four children lost; three on the ship, including their 8 year old boy John on 2 November 1863 and twin boys Thomas and Edward Collett who died in late November. A daughter Elizabeth died aged seventeen in Christchurch, New Zealand. Susan Collett was pregnant while on board the *Brother's Pride* and had her baby John three months after arriving in Christchurch. The couple died in Devonport; Susan in 1908 and John in 1914.[92]

Dunlop

David Dunlop and his wife Jeanie lost several children. Their son, Francis George, died aged 5 in 1875. At the time David was living at Palgrave Farm, St Albans. In 1877 the farm was advertised to let, my tender for a term of three years. It was a 30 acre farm with "very superior grassland" with a five room cottage, dairy, stable, orchard and outbuildings. David Dunlop was occupying the farm at the time.[93] A 13-day-old daughter, named Margaret, died at the Canal Reserve, Christchurch on 29 September 1880.[94] David Dunlop died in 1883 and was buried in Addington Cemetery.[95] Their daughter Jeanie Dunlop died at Canal Reserve Road on 11 June 1886, aged 11.[96] Jeanie died in 1918 aged 76 years old after having much tragedy in her life.[97]

Edmonds

George Edmonds and wife Martha, née Johnson, settled in Kaiapoi after arriving on the *Brother's Pride*.[98] While in quarantine, Martha gave birth to a son, named Percival Henry Edmonds on 31 December 1863. Martha died in 1889 aged a young 49.

Everett

William Everett was a farmer in Templeton in partnership with William Beckingham in 1866.[99] William and his wife Mary Ann arrived in New Zealand with three children, and had at least another five children in New Zealand.[28]

Hanson

John Edward Hanson was born in 1840 in Leeds, Yorkshire, England. He arrived on the *Brother's Pride* and was employed as a butcher on the journey. After arriving he leased ten acres at Riccarton, Christchurch from Mr C. C. Bowen, where he opened a butchery and store. He did very well and expanded the business, adding a bakery. John also started exporting bacon to Sydney and owned the Upper Riccarton flour mill. He belonged to several groups including the Riccarton Road Board, Riccarton school committee and Riccarton church choir. John was present at the consecration of Halswell church, which was done by Bishop Harper and Mr. C. C. Bowen. John married Mary Hare, who arrived by the ship Canterbury. Mary Hanson died in 1902 leaving a family of three sons and two daughters. Two sons were in the army.[100] John Edward Hanson died in 1920 aged 79 years old.[28] Hansons Lane in Riccarton, Christchurch was named after John Hanson.[101]

John Hanson

Hathaway

Mary Ann Hathaway was born at the Forest of Dean, Gloucestershire in 1846 and came to New Zealand with her parents on the *Brother's Pride*, arriving in 1863. "Those on board had the unpleasant experience of being kept in quarantine from December 14 till January 1 on their arrival in the new country." Mary Ann moved to Wellington in 1867 and married John

Futter in 1870. She lived at Thorndon except for three years living in Foxton. Her husband died in 1880 and she moved back to Thorndon. She celebrated her 90th birthday on 27 December 1936 where "a very pleasant time was spent."[102] She died in 1941 at the age of 95.[28] Mary Ann was survived by her brother, Charles Hathaway of Lower Hutt. And she had three children, eight grandchildren, and ten great-grandchildren at the time of her death.[103]

Hay

James Hoseason Hay, born about 1839 in Shetland, and his intended spouse Catherine Stout, also from Shetland, travelled to New Zealand on the *Brother's Pride*. They married at Charteris Bay (Hays Bay) on 27 January 1864; and this may have been the first marriage between Shetlanders in New Zealand. They had five children together. Catherine died in 1881. James returned to Shetland and married Jane Hay, who was his first cousin. James convinced other Shetlanders to travel back to New Zealand with him on the *Himalaya* arriving at Lyttelton in 1875. They had land at Charteris Bay and produced another three children together.[104]

Irvine

William Irvine was born in 1818 in the Shetland Islands and arrived on the *Brother's Pride* in 1863. He worked around Canterbury and then bought a farm from Mr R. H. Rhodes at Tai Tapu. He stayed there for six years. In 1870 he bought about 200 acres at Dunsandel and increased this to 600 acres over the years. William was involved with the Selwyn school committee and Presbyterian Church. The first Presbyterian service in the area was held at his house. William's second son Robert Francis Irvine, M.A. studied at Canterbury College and taught at Christ's College before moving to New South Wales in 1890, where he became the Principal of Moore College. Mrs Irvine died in about 1883 and William Irvine in 1901. They left a family of four sons and two daughters.[105]

Mr W. Irvine

Johnston(e)

Thomas Scott Johnston(e) was born in Roxburghshire, Scotland in 1854. He travelled on the *Brother's Pride* with his parents and went into station life at a young age. He worked with his father firstly at Lake Heron and then went to *Clent Hills* for fourteen years, so worked with sheep since he was a young boy. He worked for a Mr Potts and became Manager of *Hakatere*. In 1888 he was appointed Manager of *Mount Possession* by the Loan and Mercantile Company. *Mount Possession* was a run of 9000 acres freehold and 47,000 acres leasehold land. Mr Johnston(e) married Margaret Lambie in 1879, daughter of George Lambie. Thomas and Margaret had seven sons and two daughters.[106]

Mr T. S. Johnston(e)

Kirk

Henry Bland Kirk (known as Mr. H. B. Kirk) was born in Thorner, Yorkshire in 1842. His father died and his mother had to look after herself and Henry's younger brother and sister, so Henry was adopted by a pitman and his wife. Henry's adoptive parents were very kind. Henry worked in the mines in Farnley, near Leeds, where he had amazing employers. He had a wonderful childhood in general, including a fairly good education at a night school. He left for New Zealand on the *Brother's Pride* in 1863. His first job in New Zealand was making a road on Porter's Pass. He also worked at Sunnyside Asylum. He helped to put up the

Mr. H. B. Kirk

telegraph line from the Selwyn River to Arthur's Pass and helped finish the Goldney's Saddle part of the West Coast Road. He then took up brick making in Lyttelton, then moved to Christchurch and opened a brickworks on Ferry Road. He had several other businesses before moving to Timaru with his family, where he took on the old Steam Brick Works. He helped extend Timaru's sewage pipes, as well as making many other useful pottery items such as chimney pots. He was an Oddfellow and also a member of the Masonic Lodge. He married Emma Florence Canner in

1913. Henry died in 1927.[107] Austin Kirk Lane in St Martins, Christchurch was named after Austin, Kirk and Co., owners of the Farnley Brick and Tile Works.[108]

McConnell

Gordon McConnell was born in Kirkcudbrightshire, Scotland in 1838. His father owned a farm called *Blackcraig* in the parish of Balmaclellan, where Gordon was brought up. Gordon travelled to New Zealand on the *Brother's Pride* in 1863 and started shepherding on *Motunau Station*. In 1876 he bought land in Waikari Valley and settled there. He sold the land in about 1902 and retired to Waikari township. Gordon was a man of high integrity and was greatly respected and loved by all who knew him. He was not actively involved in public matters but did take an interest in the welfare of the district. He was a member of the Waikari Presbyterian Church, of which he was one of the managers. He died on 5 January 1909.[109]

McKay

Alexander and Christina McKay and 9-month-old daughter Margaret, arrived on the *Brother's Pride* in 1863. They lived in the Leeston district for about eighteen years and then moved to Ford's Road, Tinwald. Christina McKay died in 1909 aged 72, and at the time of her death there were four daughters and a son named William McKay living.[110]

MacKay

Robert MacKay was born in Rogart, Sutherlandshire in 1839 and came to New Zealand on the *Brother's Pride* with his young wife. After landing, a Mr Palmer employed Robert as a shepherd on Double Hill. In 1869, he was made manager of the whole station and moved to the main homestead. Robert "knocked the station into shape" and had a lot of the "rough work" of those days. He mustered sheep and cattle as well as ploughing the first paddocks, planting the first garden and making his own furniture. As the station was quite remote, Mrs MacKay went two years at one stage without seeing another women and had to educate her children herself. Robert gave up the job after being "tired of the back country" and took up management of *Raincliff Station* where he established a flock of merino sheep. He left in 1896 and supervised the *Opuha Gorge Station*. Bad times in the late 1890s lost MacKay his own farm called *Trentham* near Fairlie. He took over management of William Aker's large properties at Linton in the Manawatu. He started living the pioneer life again. He eventually moved to Palmerston North, where he died in June 1924.[111]

Their daughter, Jessie Mackay, became a poetess and writer. She had many books of poems published. She died in 1938 and is buried in Waimairi Cemetery, Christchurch where the first line of her last poem is written on the gravestone "Lord of the sheep in the upland ways."[112]

McKenzie

Alexander McKenzie was born in Ross-shire, Scotland in 1840 and was brought up on a farm. Alexander McKenzie came to New Zealand in the *Brother's Pride* in 1863. In his short obituary it states that the "vessel made a very long voyage to New Zealand, and no less than six deaths occurred from typhoid fever." Alexander farmed near Peel Forest for some time with English settlers before residing at Riverford, Geraldine, South Canterbury where he farmed and took up tanning. He won prizes at the Timaru, Ashburton and Christchurch shows for draught horses.[113] He died in 1915. He had celebrated the 50th anniversary of coming to NZ on the ship two years earlier and still lived a very active life.

Mr A. McKenzie

Mrs McKenzie had predeceased him 20 years earlier but he still had a family of one daughter and three sons. His family was left included Mrs R. A. Mitchell, of Gisborne, Colonel McKenzie, of Stover, Canterbury, the Rev. John McKenzie, M.A., Melbourne, and Mr Colin McKenzie, of Geraldine.[114]

McMillan

Robert McMillan was born near Glasgow, Scotland in 1861. He survived the *Brother's Pride* journey as an infant. His biography states there were 49 deaths from fever on the voyage and two after the vessel was quarantined. He first worked for Messrs Shain & McGregor in Hokitika, staying for 3 to 4 years, and then moved to Mr. D. Reese in Christchurch. He eventually went back to Hokitika and worked for the firm Sinclair & Jack for many years. He started his own partnership, McMillan & Thompson (Robert McMillan & Henry Thompson), Builders, Contractors, Undertakers and Monumental Masons, Gibson's Quay, Hokitika. Robert was into sports and was a member of all the local sports clubs.[115]

More

Colin More (sometimes incorrectly spelt Moore) was born in Inverness-shire, Scotland and went to Polmaly School. He worked in a railway workshop and then a farm before travelling to New Zealand on the *Brother's Pride* in 1863. Colin worked for Mr. Kruse in Papanui for seven years and then for Mr. Robert Duncan of Island Hill, Loburn for three years. He was the first man to be employed to clear the ground for building the Christchurch Normal School and noticed that the land was too soft there to build the school and pointed this out to the architect who redrew the plans to provide a broader foundation. He managed the estate of Mrs Daniels's *Kiplow* farm in Papanui for seventeen years before retiring to his property called *Castle Hill* in North Loburn. He married Agnes Gibb in 1889, daughter of Mr. David Gibb of Marshland. They had two daughters. Colin More died on 22 November 1901 aged fifty-six.[116]

Mr. C. More

Petherick

Mrs Elizabeth Petherick was born at St. Keverne, Cornwall. She came to New Zealand with her husband in 1863. Her husband was a goldchaser and they moved a lot, going to Adelaide, back to New Zealand, to Bendigo, and finally settling in South Australia at Wallaroo Mines. The Pethericks were among the earliest agricultural pioneers and lived there for 35 years. Mr Petherick died in about 1909 and Elizabeth in 1913 aged 78. They left behind three daughters, Mesdames W. Rodda (Green's Plains), Woodward (Victoria), and S. Davies (Lameroo), and five sons, Messrs. John (Aldgate), Richard, Charles, James, and Alfred (Green's Plains).[117]

Powell

Joseph Powell was born in Radnorshire, Wales in 1830 and came to New Zealand on the *Brother's Pride* in 1863. He stayed in Christchurch and Rangiora for a few weeks, before moving to Oxford in April 1864, where he lived until his death in 1913 at the age of eighty-three. He was one of the first settlers of Oxford but had a "quiet, retiring disposition" and was not involved in public affairs in the region. He was in bad health for about twenty years before his death and couldn't do any hard work. His golden wedding was in June 1903. His wife died in April 1912. On his death in 1913 he had a family of nine sons and daughters, forty grandchildren and a number of great grandchildren.[118]

Roberts

Frederick Roberts was born in Harrowgate, Yorkshire, England in 1826 and travelled to New Zealand on the *Brother's Pride*. His wife, Esther (née Brown), gave birth to a daughter on the ship. After arriving he farmed in different places until he settled at Springston South in 1868. It was covered in flax and raupo, which he cultivated and then had dairy and green crops on the land. All Frederick's time was spent on cultivating and improving his farm and he didn't spend time on local affairs. Frederick and Esther had nine children. Three sons and three daughters were alive in about 1903.[119]

Rountree

According to Joseph Ernest Rountree his parents Joseph and Jane Rountree (nee Smith) travelled to New Zealand on the ship *Brother's Pride*. Joseph was born in 1843 and was brought up at Cootehill in County Cavan, Ireland. He married Jane on 7 June 1863 just before leaving for New Zealand. They settled in Marshlands or Hills Road, St Albans and had six children, Johnny, Walter, Albert, Joseph, Hugh and Araminta. Araminta drowned when quite young.[120]

Scott

Mrs Joan Scott was an occasional nurse on board the *Brother's Pride*, travelling with her husband Andrew and son Thomas. Joan had the arduous task of nursing the sick and dying on board the ship along with Elizabeth Powell. Joan went on to be an evangelist in New Zealand and preached into her 70s.[121]

Scrimshaw

Henry Scrimshaw was born in Nottingham, England where he was brought up to the cabinetmaking trade. He arrived on the *Brother's Pride* in 1863 and six years later founded a business as a Cabinetmaker and Undertaker. His cabinetmaking business was situated at 87, 89 and 91 Victoria Street, and his undertaking business at 41 Durham Street South, Christchurch. He claimed to be "the oldest worker in the line, in Christchurch." He worked for a Mr R. W. Walters for a time before starting his own business. Henry made all kinds of furniture for stock or to order. His showrooms in

Victoria Street covered 8000 square feet and the goods were "tastefully displayed."[122]

Smith

Elizabeth Smith was listed in a document of prostitutes present in Christchurch in 1867. She was listed as living at Kilmore Street West, having travelled on the *Brother's Pride* as an assisted immigrant. However, there is only a Christina Smith in the original passenger list, listed under single women; no Elizabeth Smith is listed.[123]

Smith

William Tayler Smith was born in 1844 in Rothiemay, Banffshire, Scotland, son of John and Euphemia Smith (née Wilson). He travelled, aged 19, on the *Brother's Pride* to New Zealand, following his brother Hay who had arrived in January 1863. His other brothers, George and Charles, followed in 1864. He worked on the West Coast goldfields from 1863 to 1867, and then changed his profession to bullock driver. He worked on farms in the Mt Somers/Staveley area including the farm *Buccleuch*. He married Hannah Graham on 26 May 1869 in Lyttelton and settled at a property called *Birchlands* where they had a transport business using

Hannah and William Smith at Birchlands, 1898. (detail)

bullocks and horses. They had 11 children, 7 daughters and 4 sons. He died in 1902 after being lost overboard from the *Zealandia* between Napier and Auckland. It appears someone may have robbed him and pushed him overboard.[124]

Sparks

William John Sparks was born in London in 1851 and travelled to New Zealand at the age of 12 on the *Brother's Pride*. He joined the staff of the Christchurch Museum in 1870 as a junior and was appointed to a taxidermist position in 1883. William was also a member of the Philosophical Institution of Canterbury.[125]

Thomson

Mr. P. Thomson.

Peter Thomson was born near Kinross, Scotland in 1839 and worked with his father John Thomson and his brothers on their farm located near the Bridge of Earn, Perthshire. The family travelled to New Zealand on the *Brother's Pride* in 1863. Peter's first job in New Zealand was with farmer James Gammack at Springston, where he stayed for three years. Peter then became a farmer at Leeston and moved to Winton in 1870 where his brother and father were residing. Their farm was called *Spring Burn Farm*. Peter was involved in the local community, being a trustee of the Winton racecourse and director of the Farmers' United Agency Company. He was also a member of the Southland County Council. Peter married in 1876 to Julia Graham Henderson,[28] daughter of Walter Henderson and they had seven children. Peter died in June 1894.[126] Julia Graham Thomson died in 1937 aged 81.

Torrens

James Torrens was born in Peeble-shire, Scotland in about 1840 and travelled to New Zealand on the *Brother's Pride* in 1863. He bought land in Spreydon (known as Tankerville at the time), which he farmed and lived at until his death. In later years he bred draught horses. He was interested in agriculture and people turned to him when there were problems with horses and no veterinary surgeon available. He became ill for a week before dying on 3 July 1897. There is currently a Torrens Road in Spreydon, Christchurch.[127]

Trigg

Absalom Trigg was born in Drybrook, Gloucestershire in about 1831. He married Hannah Cowmeadow, who was born in Drybrook in 1834. They emigrated to New Zealand on the *Brother's Pride*. On the way, Hannah gave birth to twin boys, but on the 11 November 1863 one died on board the ship. Tragically, Hannah also died on board the ship. The other twin was lost while in quarantine and buried at Camp Bay.

Absalom married two other times, first to Annie Gundy (who may have been a fellow passenger on the ship) and then Esther Arnold, and had many children with both wives. In 1870 his name was in the Daily Southern Cross newspaper as having shares in a gold mining company in the Thames area, so it appears he may have been a gold chaser.[128] He lived in Tararu near Thames and Little River, Canterbury and died in Okaihau, Northland, New Zealand in 1900.

Voice

George and James Voice (often incorrectly spelt Voyce) were brothers who travelled from the Forest of Dean, Gloucestershire on the *Brother's Pride* with their families.

James and Sarah lost their son Henry, aged 21 months, on the voyage.[47] Sarah was pregnant on the voyage and had a daughter named Sarah Ann on 19 December 1863 while in quarantine at Camp Bay.

George and Elizabeth Voice expected that they would have plenty of time before the birth of their child to get to New Zealand. However their daughter, named Mary Ann,[129] was born in quarantine on 27 December 1863.[54] When the ship went into Cape Town, George went onshore and bought some oranges which Elizabeth almost lived on for the rest of the journey![59] Once in Christchurch each couple had many children. George worked on the Lyttelton Tunnel for quite a while before moving the family to Makikihi near Waimate, where they lived near the bush. They then moved to Templeton. George and Elizabeth had 7 daughters and 4 sons.[59]

In 1873 James Voice was a wheelwright at Templeton.[130] The family lived on the main road next to Kissell's store.[129] In 1882 he was a blacksmith living near the Templeton Railway station.[131] He worked there with his sons Tom and Joseph.[129] Joseph Henry was born to James and Sarah in 1867, his middle name after his older brother who had died on the voyage.[28] James Voice died at Templeton in 1900 aged 64.[132] George Voice died in 1915.[133]

Walker

William Walker was born in Galston, Ayreshire, Scotland. He married Agnes Stewart. In 1863 they boarded the *Brother's Pride* for New Zealand with their two children Grace, about 3, and James who was 8 months old when they arrived. William took up work at Anderson's Foundry, as he had trained as a blacksmith. He worked there for ten years before buying land at Dunsandel, both farming the land and setting up a blacksmith shop.[134] William and Agnes had a family of seven children.

William & Agnes Walker and children Grace & little James c. 1864

William passed away in 1893 aged 57,[135] and Agnes in 1900 aged 69.[136]

Whitelaw

John Whitelaw was born in Quanelheads, Shotts, Lanarkshire, Scotland in 1837. He was a joiner and carpenter, and in 1860, after working hard and obtaining a responsible position with the firm of Messrs McIntyre and Jack of Glasgow, John married a daughter of Dr. George Willison of Prestopans. While in Scotland he was a member of the Duke Street U.P. Church and superintendant of one of its large Sunday schools. In 1863 he sailed on the *Brother's Pride* to Lyttelton and wrote one of the only known diaries for the journey. On arrival, he worked as a joiner and carpenter for Mr McGuire and Mr Joseph Bailey. He tried his luck with the Nelson gold diggings but didn't have much success. He then went to Prebbleton to start business on his own and then moved to Kaiapoi where he started flaxmilling. He leased Stronyer's mill, which became Ohoka flourmills. After only being in the milling business for a week his right hand was drawn into the machinery and permanently injured. He then worked as a clerk for Daniel Reese and then a more responsible position with James Goss. In about 1872 he entered the Provincial Government's engineer's office as a draughtsman, his boss being Mr Thornton, C.E. When the provinces were abolished, John was retained under the General Government to carry out works. He did this under supervision of the Hon.

W. Rolleston, superintendant, who spoke highly of John's integrity and ability. John had charge of the West Coast road and in 1878 began business as an architect and valuer. He designed part of the Sydenham public school and the Sydenham Presbyterian church. Then, in 1879, he was appointed as a valuer for the Christchurch City Council. He was a member of many clubs, churches and associations. On his death he left a widow and five children. He was living at Brougham Street, Sydenham at the time of his death in 1904.[137] At his funeral at Addington Cemetery many wreaths were received including one from about 20 shipmates from *Brother's Pride* who attended his funeral.[138]

Williamson

John and Marjory A. Williamson were from Hardwall Delting, Sheltand Islands before travelling to New Zealand on the *Brother's Pride*. They had both been widowed and married each other a year before travelling. Marjory had children, Thomas and Agnes, and John had children, named John and Catherine. They had two more children in Christchurch, New Zealand, Mary Elizabeth and Andrew.[104]

Woodhouse

William Woodhouse was born at Lynn, Norfolk, England and came to New Zealand in the *Brother's Pride* in 1863. He had a sudden death at age fifty-nine; he was described as an "elderly man." He had been employed at Vincent's Brewery and lived at Aynsley Street, Sydenham. On 5 June 1898, William went to the Sydenham Working Men's Club at about noon and asked for a glass of beer and sat down in a chair to drink it. People in the club noticed him looking "peculiar" and sent for Dr Thomas, but just as he arrived William Woodhouse died. He left a family of eleven children and a widow.[139]

Passenger Lists

The following lists have been transcribed directly from the passenger lists of steerage passengers, with cabin passengers taken from newspaper articles. There were no cabin passengers listed in the newspapers for the *Brother's Pride*. Corrections were made after research was done on the passengers. The original transcriptions are in square brackets beside the correct spelling.

Bahia Passengers 1863[140]				
Crew				
Surname	*Given Name*	*Age*	*Location*	*Occupation/ Notes*
Le Fanu	Capt. Peter			Commander
Chief Cabin				
Surname	*Given Name*	*Age*	*Location*	*Occupation/ Notes*
Warren	Mrs			
Warren	Miss			
Thomson	Miss			
Thomson	Miss			
Rouse	Miss			
Malyon	Miss			
Innes	Mr			
Innes	Mrs			
Second Cabin				
Surname	*Given Name*	*Age*	*Location*	*Occupation/ Notes*
Rose	Mr			
Rose	Mrs			
Ross	Mr			
Ross	Mrs			
Scarcombe	Mr			
Scarcombe	Mrs			
Dodd	Mr			
Dodd	Mrs			
Dodd	Child			

Dodd	Child			
Moffatt	Mr			
Cambridge	Mr John Miles			
Smith	Mr			
Steerage				
Unnamed				*Press* 9 Dec 1863 says "and two others in steerage"
Unnamed				

Brother's Pride Passengers 1863[47]

Crew

Surname	Given Name	Age	Location	Occupation/ Notes
Glendinning	Alexander			Captain
Dermott	Fitzherbert			Surgeon
Jameson	Mr.			Chief Officer
Shepherd	James			Second Mate *Married Jane McWilliam*

Chief Cabin

Unknown as not listed in the newspapers				

Second Cabin

Surname	Given Name	Age	Location	Occupation/ Notes
Ellery	Mrs			
	John	13		*Son of Mrs Ellery.* **Died on ship**

Government Immigrants

Married Couples

Surname	Given Name	Age	Location	Occupation/ Notes
Anderson	Andrew	55	Shetland	Farm Labourer
	Martha	47		
	Margaret	21		*T/F single women*
	William	18		*T/F single women*
	Robert	6		
Bailey	Samuel	34	Gloucestershire	Farm Labourer
	Ann	36		

	John	10		
	William	9		
	Charles	7		
	Thomas	6		
	Frank	4		
	Joseph	3		*Died aboard ship*
	George	Infant		
Baker	Walter	33	Gloucestershire	Farm Labourer
	Jane	43		
	Thomas	25		*T/F single men*
Banton	Henry	22	Cheshire	Farm Labourer
	Mary	23		
	Henry	Infant		
Bayliss [Baylis]	James	47	Herefordshire	Farm Labourer
	Elizabeth	40		
	Sarah	17		*T/F single women*
	Thomas	15		*T/F single men*
	James	11		
	John	8		
	William	6		
	Henry	3		
Birch	John	35	Cornwall	Mason
	Martha	30		
	John	11		
	Elizabeth Ann	7		
	Benjamin	4		
	Martha Jane	2		
	James Edward	4 mths		*Died on voyage*
Bonnett	Henry	33	Suffolk	Bricklayer
	Eliza	30		*Died on voyage*
	Jane	4		

	George	15 mths		*Died on voyage*
	Son	Infant		*Born on ship*
Brassington	William	23	Nottingham-shire	Mason
	Ellen	21		
	Florence	3		
	Mary Ellen	1		*Died on voyage*
Brooks	William	33	Cheshire	Farm Labourer
	Ann (Fanny)	43		*Died on voyage*
	Sarah Jane	7		
	Ellen Anne	4		
Brown	John	27	Fifeshire	Farm Labourer
	Janet	28		*Died on voyage*
	Robert	7		*Died on voyage*
	Margaret	5		
	David	3		*Died on voyage*
	Agnes	2		*Died on voyage*
	Son	Infant		*Born on ship* *Died on voyage*
Campbell	John	27	Sutherland	Shepherd
	Elizabeth	17		
Chester	George	32	Cornwall	Farm Labourer
	Grace	33		
	William Henry	4		
Cole	Charles	28	Gloucestershire	Farm Labourer
	Elizabeth	30		
	Robert	10		
	Mary	8		*Died on voyage*
	Fanny	5		
	John	Infant		*Died on voyage*
Collett	John	36	Worcestershire	Carpenter
	Susan	35		
	Mary Ann	10		

	John	8		*Died on voyage*
	Sarah Jane	6		
	Thomas	2		*Died on voyage*
	Edward	2		*Died on voyage*
	Elizabeth	1		
Crosbie	Andrew	45	Dumfrieshire	Farm Labourer *Died on voyage*
	Agnes	39		
	Agnes	11		
	Jane	10		
	Andrew	8		*Died on voyage*
Crowley	Cornelius	29	Middlesex	Carpenter
	Catherine	30		
	George	10		
	Cornelius	8		
	Margaret	5		
	Catherine	4		
	Josiah	2		
	Mary	7 Mths		
Dunlop	David	26	Ayrshire	Ploughman
	Jeanie	22		
	David	2		
Edmonds	George	25	Kent	Labourer
	Martha	24		
	George	5		
	Charles	Infant		
Everett [Everitt]	William	34	Gloucestershire	Farm Labourer
	Mary Ann	27		
	Elizabeth	10		
	Moses	6		
	Aaron	Infant		
Grainger	Matthew B.	25	Yorkshire	Farrier

	Martha	22		
	Thomas	10		
	Matthew	3		
Gundy	John	44	Monmouthshire	Farm Labourer
	Sarah Ann	44		
	John	21		*T/F single men*
	Elizabeth	19		*T/F single women*
	Sarah Ann	17		*T/F single women* **Died on voyage**
	Walter	15		*T/F single men*
	Annie	13		*T/F single women*
	Harriet	11		
	James	9		
	Mary Ann	7		
	Thomas Albert	4		
Gunn	Richard	39	Cornwall	Farm Labourer
	Mary	38		
Hathaway	George	46	Gloucestershire	Farm Labourer
	Sarah	46		
	William	18		*T/F single men*
	Mary Anne	16		*T/F single women*
	Sarah	14		*T/F single women*
	George	12		*T/F single men*
	Charles	8		
	Louisa	6		
	Benjamin	4		
Hathaway	David	25	Gloucestershire	Farm Labourer
	Milbrough	30		*(female)*
	Felix	4		
	David Jnr.	1		

Passenger Lists

	Son	Infant		***Born on ship Died in Quarantine***
Hawkins	George	34	Gloucestershire	Farm Labourer
	Alice	28		
	James	7		
	Charles	4		
	William	2		
	Samuel	8 mth		***Died on voyage***
Helem [Helm]	George	33	Caithness-shire	Shepherd
	Isabella	33		
	William	9		
	Elizabeth	7		
	Peter	5		
	Jessie	2		***Died on voyage***
	Son	Infant		***Born on ship***
Irvine	William	45	Shetland	Farm Labourer
	Joan	33		
	Ann	11		
	Alexander	7		
	Margaret	4		
	Robert F.	1		
Johnston(e)	James	27	Roxburghshire	Shepherd
	Mary	26		
	Thomas	8		
	Margaret	4		
	Mary	2		
	John	9 mths		***Died on voyage***
Jowett	John	36	Yorkshire	Farm Labourer
	Sarah	45		
	Nathan	16		*T/F single men*
	Hannah	14		*T/F single women (note "Mrs*

					Johnston Birch Yard (Baileys)")
King	Thomas Paull	38	Suffolk	Farm Labourer	
	Elizabeth	34			
	Georgina	14			*T/F single women*
	Thomas	11			
	Alice	10			
	Frederick	6			
MacKay [McKay]	Robert	24	Sutherland	Shepherd	
	Elizabeth	21			
	Walter	7 mths			
McKay	Alexander	24	Caithness-shire	Farm Labourer	
	Christina	27			
	Margaret	9 mths			
	Daughter	Infant			***Born on ship***
McLaughlan	Archibald	33	Donegal	*Schoolmaster on ship*	
	Jane Elizabeth	33	Denbighshire	*Matron on ship*	
	Son	Infant			***Born on ship***
McLennan	Duncan	29	Morayshire	Farm Labourer	
	Ellen	27	Elginshire		
McMillan	John	27	Lanarkshire	Farm Labourer	
	Catherine	27			
	Margaret	4			***Died on voyage***
	Robert	2			
	Andrew	13 mths			***Died on voyage***
McMillan	Donald	30	Sutherland	Shepherd	
	Jessie	26			
Mason	John	28	Lanarkshire	Ploughman	
	Eliza	26			
Monro	Robert	22	Sutherland	Shepherd	

	Jane	26		
Nicholls	Henry	23	Cornwall	Farm Labourer
	Elizabeth	23		
	Benjamin	3 mth		*Died on voyage*
Norbury	Peter	25	Lancashire	Labourer
	Mary	25		
	Edith B.	3		*Died on voyage*
Odgers	James	28	Cornwall	Carpenter
	Elizabeth	34		
	Emma	2		
Petherick	William	29	Cornwall	Farm Labourer
	Elizabeth	27		
Powell	Richard	24	Gloucestershire	Farm Labourer *Travelled with G. Hathaway* *Died on voyage*
	Elizabeth	?		
	Eda[39]	2		*Died on voyage*[39]
Powell	Joseph	32	Herefordshire	Farm Labourer
	Mary	29		
	Lewis	9		
	Thomas	7		
	William	6		*Died on voyage*
	Aaron	4		
	Mary Ann	9 mths		
Rosser	John	22	Gloucestershire	Farm Labourer *Died on voyage*
	Sophia	22		*Died on voyage*
	Charles	Infant		Was orphaned at 12 to 18 months old.[37]
Round	Elijah	39	Staffordshire	Labourer
	Ann Maria	38		
	Ebenezer	17		T/F single men

	Emma	15		*T/F single women*
	Amelia	13		*T/F single women*
	Mary	11		
	William	7		
	Hannah	4		
	Ann Maria	2		
Scott	Andrew	35	Roxburgh	Carpenter
	Joan	34		*Nurse on ship*
	Thomas	10		
Scrimshaw	Henry	25	Nottinghamshire	Carpenter
	Eliza	22		
	Cornelius	3		
	William Henry	1		**Died aboard ship**
Sparks [Sparkes]	William	34	Middlesex	Joiner
	Rebecca	35		
	William	11		
	Rebecca	9		
	Frederick	6		
	Emily	4		
	Mary Ann	8 mths		
Stout	William	29	Shetland	Farm Labourer
	Barbara	29		
	Son	Infant		**Born on ship**
	Inga	57		*T/F single women*
	Margaret	34		*T/F single women*
	Catherine	27		*T/F single women*
	Mary M.	21		*T/F single women*
	Helen	19		*T/F single women*

Thomas	Matthew	21	Gloucestershire	Farm Labourer
	Charlotte	18		
	S. M.	Infant		*Died on voyage*
Trigg	Absalom	32	Gloucestershire	Farm Labourer
	Anna (Hannah)	28		*Died on voyage*
	Twin boy	Infant		*Born on ship Died in Quarantine*
	Twin boy	Infant		*Born on ship Died on voyage*
Voice [Voyce]	James	25	Gloucestershire	Carpenter
	Sarah	25		
	William	3		*According to a family story, he was crippled on the voyage*[141]
	Henry	21 mths		*Died on voyage*
Voice [Voyce]	George	28	Gloucestershire	Farm Labourer
	Elizabeth	20		
Wallace	George	30	Ayrshire	Mason
	Janet	31		
	James	7		
	Andrew	6		
	Janet	2		
Webb	William	33	Gloucestershire	Farm Labourer
	Mary	31		
	Henry	12		*T/F single men*
	Mary	7		
	William	5		
	Thomas	3		*Died on voyage*
	Clara	10 mths		*Died on voyage*
Whitelaw	John	26	Lanarkshire	Joiner
	Georgina	29		
	George	3		

		Mths		
Williams	James	29	Cornwall	Farm Labourer
	Phillipa	29		
Williams	Henry	41	Gloucestershire	Farm Labourer
	Charlotte	39		**Died on voyage**
	Eliza	16		*T/F single women*
	Pamela	14		*T/F single women*
	Joseph S.	12		*T/F single men*
	Harry P.	2		
	William	Infant		
Williamson	John	35	Shetland	Farm Labourer
	Marjory A.	36		
	Thomas	8		
	Agnes	6		
	John	4		
	Catherine	1		
Wilson	John	36	Lanarkshire	Farm Labourer
	Margaret	36		
	Cecilia	14		*T/F single women*
	Alexander	9		
	John	2		
Young	John	24	Gloucestershire	Farm Labourer
	Eliza	23		

Single Men

Surname	*Given Name*	*Age*	*Location*	*Occupation/ Notes*
Anderson	John	22	Lanarkshire	Ploughman *Travelled with J. McMillan*
Anderson	William	18	Shetland	Farm Labourer
Austin	William	22	Yorkshire	Farm Labourer
Aylward	Richard	13	Waterford	

Baker	Thomas	25	Gloucestershire	Farm Labourer
Baylis	Thomas	15	Gloucestershire	Labourer
Bee	Isaac	25	Lincolnshire	Labourer
Benfield	Henry	21	Gloucestershire	Farm Labourer *Travelled with H. Williams*
Benfield	William	14	Gloucestershire	
Beyers	James	27	Dumfries-shire	Carpenter
Burnett	Alexander	20	Aberdeenshire	Farm Labourer
Campbell	Malcolm	27	Inverness	Ploughman
Crichton	Thomas	18	Perthshire	Ploughman
Cumming	John	21	Fifeshire	Ploughman
Cutler	George	24	Gloucestershire	Farm Labourer *Travelled with J. Young*
Eaton	John	34	Worcestershire	Gardener
Eaton	Joseph	19	Worcestershire	Gardener
Edwards	Eli	18	Gloucestershire	Farm Labourer *Travelling with Baker family*
Ferguson	Peter	26	Kirkcudbright-shire	Ploughman *Travelled with Crosbie*
Foden	James	19	Lancashire	Farm Labourer
Fraser	John	26	Ross-shire	Ploughman
Fraser	William	27	Ross-shire	Ploughman
Gray	John	22	Ross-shire	Ploughman
Gundy	John	21	Gloucestershire	Farm Labourer
Gundy	Walter	15	Gloucestershire	Farm Labourer
Gunn	William	25	Sutherland	Farm Labourer
Hanson	John Edward	21	Yorkshire	Labourer
Hay	James	24	Shetland	Farm Labourer *Travelled with W. Stout*
Howell	Thomas	33	Gloucestershire	Farm Labourer *Travelled with D. Hathaway*
Johnson	Jesse	20	Yorkshire	Farm Labourer

Johnston	George	16	Down	Farm Labourer
Jowett	Nathan	16	Yorkshire	Labourer
Kirk	Henry	20	Lancashire	Farm Labourer
Lloyd	Emanual	26	Somersetshire	Farm Labourer
Lloyd	Thomas	20	Somersetshire	Farm Labourer
McConnell	Gordon	25	Kirkcudbright-shire	Shepherd *Travelled with Crosbie*
McKenzie	Alexander	24	Ross-shire	Farm Labourer
McMillan	Ewan	28	Inverness	Farm Labourer
McMillan	John	31	Inverness	Ploughman
Middlemiss	John	22	Yorkshire	Farm Labourer
More [Moore]	Colin	22	Inverness	Ploughman
Morton	James	20	Fifeshire	Ploughman
O'Neill	John	28	Armagh	Labourer
Round	Ebenezer	17	Staffordshire	Labourer
Peebles	Andrew	22	Perthshire	Farm Labourer
Protheroe	John	21	Hertfordshire	Blacksmith
Protheroe	William	19	Hertfordshire	Farm Labourer
Reid	James	24	Aberdeen	Carpenter
Richards	George	30	Gloucestershire	Farm Labourer
Shelton	Isaac	33	Nottingham-shire	Farm Labourer **Died on voyage**
Tait	James	26	Perthshire	Farm Labourer
Thomas	William	24	Gloucestershire	Farm Labourer *Travelled with M. Thomas*
Thomson	Peter	?	Scotland?	Farm Labourer
Torrens	James	23	Peeble-shire	Farm Labourer *Travelled with W. Irvine*
Tulloch	John	19	Shetland	Farm Labourer
Tulloch	Magnus	55	Shetland	
Tulloch	William	18	Shetland	Farm Labourer
Wallace	Robert	25	Ayrshire	Mason
Webb	Henry	12	Gloucestershire	

Surname	Given Name	Age	Location	Occupation/Notes
Williams	Edward	?	Gloucestershire	Labourer *Travelled with A. Trigg*
Williams	Joseph	12	Gloucestershire	

Single Women

Surname	Given Name	Age	Location	Occupation/Notes
Abbott	Jane	19	Middlesex	Needlewoman
Anderson	Margaret	21	Shetland	Farm Servant *Died on voyage*
Angus	Isabella M.	29	Aberdeenshire	Dom. Servant
Aylward	Martha B.	36	Aberdeenshire	Dom. Servant
Aylward	Richard	13		T/F single men
Aylward	Mary Ann	11		
Aylward	William	9		
Aylward	Martha	7		
Baylis	Sarah	17	Gloucestershire	Dom. Servant
Beaman	Clara	17	Salop	Dom. Servant
Benfield	Elizabeth	34	Gloucestershire	Needlewoman *Married H. Williams*
Benfield	William	14		T/F single men
Benfield	Amos	10		
Benfield	Richard	7		
Brown	Janet	25	Lanarkshire	Dairy-woman *Died on voyage*
Carter	Elizabeth J.	14	Cornwall	
Eaton	Frances	28	Lancashire	Dom. Servant *Died on voyage*
Eaton	Harriet	21	Worcestershire	Dressmaker
Garvan	Annie	23	Ayrshire	Dom. Servant
Gundy	Annie	13	Gloucestershire	Dom. Servant
Gundy	Elizabeth	19	Gloucestershire	Dom. Servant
Gundy	Sarah	17	Gloucestershire	Dom. Servant *Died on voyage*
Gunn	Johann	28	Sutherland	Dom. Servant
Hathaway	Mary Ann	16	Gloucestershire	Dom. Servant

Hathaway	Sarah	14	Gloucestershire	
Helem [Helm]	Janet	19	Roxburgh	Dom. Servant
Jowett	Hannah	14	Yorkshire	
Keith	Mary	23	Argyleshire	Tailoress
King	Georgina	14	Suffolk	
McWilliam	Jane	21	Aberdeenshire	Dairy-woman *Married James Shepherd*
Mewes	Jane F	18	Surrey	Dom. Servant
Moffatt	Elizabeth	18	Dumfries-shire	Dom. Servant
Moffatt	Mary	23	Dumfries-shire	Dom. Servant
Munro	Andrina	19	Sutherland	Dom. Servant
Pouncey	Susan	?	Middlesex	Dom. Servant
Round	Amelia	13	Staffordshire	
Round	Emma	15	Staffordshire	Dom. Servant
Scott	Louisa	28	Nottingham-shire	Dom. Servant
Smith	Christina	17	Aberdeenshire	Dom. Servant
Stout	Catherine	27	Shetland	Dairy-woman
Stout	Helen	19	Shetland	Dairy-woman
Stout	Inge	57	Shetland	
Stout	Margaret	34	Shetland	Dairy-woman *Died on voyage*
Stout	Mary Ann	21	Shetland	Dairy-woman
Sutherland	Ann	23	Sutherland	Dom. Servant
Tulloch	Elizabeth	26	Shetland	Dairy-woman
Tulloch	Margaret	11		
Williams	Eliza	16	Gloucestershire	Dom. Servant
Williams	Pamela	14	Gloucestershire	
Wilson	Cecilia	14	Lanarkshire	

Confirmed Passengers (not on original passenger list)

Surname	*Given Name*	*Age*	*Location*	*Occupation/ Notes*
Walker	William			Confirmed by family.[134] Also signed petition.

		Agnes			
		Grace	3		
		James	8 mths		

Unconfirmed Passengers/Crew					
Surname		*Given Name*	*Age*	*Location*	*Occupation/ Notes*
Beaton		Niel	27	Scotland	Was charged with larceny in 1873. Named as a master mariner, so was probably crew on the ship.[142]
Cole		George			Signed the Petition
Hamilton		Henrietta			Possibly a cabin passenger[39]
		Daughter			***Born on ship.***
Hayden		Lewes			Signed the Petition
Jackson		George			Signed the Petition
John		Edwin			Signed the Petition
Kanting		Joseph			Signed the Petition
McKenna		James			Signed the Petition
McMillan		Evan			Signed the Petition
McWilliam		Margaret	4		***Died on ship*** Her parents are not mentioned.[39]
Roberts		Frederick			Possibly cabin passengers[39]
		Esther			
		Daughter			***Born on ship***
Rogers		George			Signed the Petition
Rountree		Joseph			Story passed down the family by son Joseph
Rountree		Jane			

					Ernest Rountree.[120]
Smith	Elizabeth				Listed in 1867 as a prostitute who was an assisted immigrant on the *Brother's Pride*.[123]
Smith	William Tayler	19		Scotland	From family website.[124]
Walker	James				Signed the Petition
Confirmed Stowaways from the Cape of Good Hope[45]					
Rae	Richard				
Maloney	Thomas				
Chapman	William				

Appendix

The *Brother's Pride* Petition[65]

Signed by the Undersigned

John Whitelaw	James Voice
Andrew Anderson	David Hathaway
John Masson [Mason]	C. Crowley
William Irvine	John Young
John Williamson	William Sparkes
Andrew Scott	Henry Bonnett
James Johnson	Elizabeth King
John Brown	John Gundy
William Walker	Henry Banton
John Clott [Collett]	G. Edmonds
Henry Nicholls	Wm Brooks
James Rodgers [Odgers]	Harry Benfield
James Williams	George Rogers
Henry Scrimshaw	George Cutter
Robert Mackay	William Benfield
Donald McMillan	Eli Edwards
Elijah Round	Thomas Howell
Peter Norbury	Edward Williams
George Helem	James McKenna
Alexander McKay	William Protheroe
William Pitherick [Petherick]	Nathan Jewell [Jowett]
Richard Gunn	Jack Protheroe
George Voice	Joseph Kanting
John Birch	Edwin Johns
George Chester	James Tait
Henry Williams	James Walker
Lewes Hayden	John Gay [Gray]
George Hawkins	Joseph Eaton
William Webb	John Eaton
John Gundy	John Powell

James Baylis [Bayliss]	Malcolm Campbell
Joseph Powell	Alexander Mackay
William Everett	John McMillan
Samuel Bailey	Evan McMillan
Absalom Trigg	Colin More [Moore]
George Cole	Robert Wallace
Matthew Thomas	George Jackson
T. P. King	

Note: names in brackets are different spellings of the surnames determined through research by the author.

Passenger Statements

While the immigrants were at Camp Bay they made Statements, of which some minutes were taken:[41]

John Whitelaw

states:

I am an assisted immigrant per *"Brother's Pride"*. I was only asked the names and ages of my family when the immigrants were inspected at Gravesend, and this was about the amount of medical examination that generally took place.

Our cook was sent ashore as incompetent, on the English coast, his place was supplied first by two blacksmiths; they soon gave it up. Then by two of the sailors, who also gave it up. For some days then the galley fire was kept up by a stowaway, the passengers cooking for themselves, but afterwards the Captain appointed a man, who did his duty fairly – this was after we had been about 3 weeks out.

After the 6th September when we were in 4° 12 Lat, the sheep were allowed to run loose upon the deck; their pen being occupied by pigs brought from a ship spoken. After leaving the Cape, the 6 sheep and a goat taken on board there were also kept loose, making the deck constantly filthy.

I heard many complaints about wet berths; mine was dry.

We left the Cape on the 23rd October; on the 19th November, our medical comforts were exhausted with the exception of gin.

No regular inspections were held as to the cleanliness of persons and berths. To the best of my belief, people were allowed to do just as they liked.

Women and men were placed in the forward hospital, in the single men's compartment. The poop Hospital (among the females) was never used as such but appropriated by the doctor.

The doctor was generally attentive to the sick; since leaving the Cape, the amount of sickness was sufficient to occupy his time.

The passengers, on crossing the line had money demanded of them by the sailors for drink under penalty of being shaved; this was done with the sanction of the Captain and Surgeon.

I cannot say that the Captain was in the habit of being drunk. I could not tell certainly. I am sure I saw him once the worse for liquor. This was on the 13th November: it was then blowing very hard, almost a storm: he was ordering the hatches to be battered down.

George Hathaway

I was a constable on board the *"Brother's Pride."* The Government Inspector at Gravesend only looked at us and asked our names. I did not see him make any particular inspection of any one.

The 'tween decks was cleaned and scraped on an average about twice a week: the upper deck was mostly wet, and kept very dirty by the dogs. The sheep were also loose about the deck and sometimes the pigs.

The deck was very leaky – my berth was mostly wet.

I had to attend to the single girls; the Matron was very attentive, and strict with them.

I was appointed Constable by the Captain and doctor. There were no regulations as to airing bedding and people did as they liked.

Peter Norbury

Am a married immigrant by the *"Brother's Pride"* My wife was prematurely confined on board. I have seen the doctor in liquor; it was at the time my child died. He was not so bad but that he knew what he was about. The deck was very leaky over my berth – our compartment was not kept very clean; boxes were stowed under the berths, and there was a quantity of rubbish always there. We were on the starboard side, opposite the mizzen mast. No proper attention was paid to keeping the decks clean. There was frequently a great stench from the use of chamber utensils in the 'tween decks. I have often been obliged to get up and go on deck on account of it. I was shaved on the line, by force: the captain and doctor were present.

Andrew Scott

I am a married immigrant per *"Brother's Pride."* I was shaved on the line, against my will. The Captain was standing by – I offered to give the crew money to release me, but was refused. When my wife was lying sick in the hospital, I had to pay 2/6 a bottle for porter for her: early in the voyage I had 4 or 5 bottles given me for her by the doctor. She was then nursing. I never got any under 1/6 a bottle. My wife was put in the forward hospital – men, women and children were put there together. The part of the 'tween decks where my family was, was kept pretty clean. The Captain did not appear to have much control over the sailors.

James Johnson

Married immigration per *"Brother's Pride."* There were six in our compartment. We refused to pay money to the sailors to avoid being shaved on the line. The doctor said "he would make it the worse for us." A little boy of mine died on the passage. He was 17 days ill. During that time he had 3 oz of wine given him, three times, but nothing else in the form of arrowroot, sago, preserved milk or other invalid diet.

John Brown

Married immigrant per *"Brother's Pride."* On the night of the 9th November, my wife was taken in labor: the doctor was the worse for drink. I had to go three times for him, and the child was born before he came. The string which was put upon the navel came off that night and the child bled very much. The doctor refused that night to examine one of my children who was ill, saying that he had too much to do. He refused also the next morning but afterward took the child into the hospital where he died at 4 am the following morning.

My children were not kept clean while in the Hospital – the doctor refused to allow Mrs Scott to come into the Hospital to attend to them. A man used to sleep with the sick nurse while in the Hospital. She has no husband. The man has slept with her since she has been here (Camp Bay).

I was compelled to pay money to prevent my being shaved on the line. The crew were allowed to come between decks at all hours. The night my child died the doctor could not be found.

About the middle of the week before we landed a testimonial was carried round to be signed by the passengers for the Captain and Doctor. I refused to sign it. The day after this the Doctor came down very much the worse for drink and wanted to know why I did not do so.

Robert McKay

Married immigration per *"Brother's Pride."* I did not get sufficiency of preserved milk or other extras for my child, mentioned in my contract ticket. We were worse off for medical comforts after leaving the Cape than before. I had to pay 1/6, 2/.

And 2/6 a bottle for porter from the Steward.

Joseph Torren[s]

Married immigrant per *"Brother's Pride"* on the 2nd Sep a little boy of mine 6 ½ years old was taken very ill about midday. I took him to the doctor; he said he thought there was not much the matter. The child continued getting worse till night. The doctor looked at him, and said he would be all right by morning. About 4 in the morning he was much worse. I went to call the doctor; it was an hour before I could make him hear. When he came, the child was dying. He expired about 5 minutes after. The doctor denied having seen him before at all. I had nothing given me for the child. I believe the doctor was not sober in the evening when he came to see him.

Charles Cole

Married immigrant. I had a child ill a fortnight before she was put in the Hospital. All that time I got no allowance of medical comforts for her. She was put into the Hospital into a bed from which a little girl had been taken, dead about an hour before. The bed had never been changed. I saw the mark in the bed where the body had been lying.

My little boy died from want, just before the vessel arrived; the doctor had no medical comforts to give him.

John Collett

Married immigrant per *"Brother's Pride"*. I have lost 3 children on the voyage. The decks were always very wet. When we were crossing the line, six or seven sailors came into my berth and demanded money.

John Mason

Married Immigrant per *Brother's Pride*. On the 5th December my wife miscarried. I went for the doctor. When he came down, he was the worse for drink. He could not keep his balance.

Mrs Mason

This is quite true he fell into the bunk where I was. He smelt strongly of gin.

Richard Gunn

On crossing the line, I was thrown in the water by the 2nd Mate.

Samuel Bailey

I lost a child on the voyage. It got no attendance till just before its death.

Evidence as to conduct of ship *"Brother's Pride"* Taken before the Executive Council at the Government Buildings on Friday the 15th day of January 1864.[75]

Present: The President
The Provincial Solicitor
Mr Ross
Mr Stevens

Messrs Donald & Rouse, Immigration Commissioners. The Captain & Doctor of the Ship. Mr C. W. Turner attended on behalf of the charterers.

Petition from passengers preferring allegation and praying for enquiry was read No. 1.

Richard Hamilton examined

I was a Cabin passenger on board *"Brother's Pride"*. I had not much opportunity of seeing state of Emigrants. I have not been in the Hospital. I saw some of the Emigrants convalescent. I don't know the exact number of deaths that took place. Dogs were loose at times. I don't know how many. I saw sheep and pigs loose on deck but not often. There was shaving on the line, some got shaved for the fun of it. I don't remember seeing any of the Immigrants shaved against their will. The shaving was carried on under the poop. The upper decks were washed every morning and kept constantly swept. I never saw sailors down in the 'tween decks. The Captain and Doctor went down every morning. I can't say whether Emigrants were mustered on Sunday. I have no complaints to make against the ship. I heard no complaints of bedding being kept wet by leaking of decks for days, it might have been for weeks. There were pens for sheep and pigs on the main deck. They were let out occasionally when the decks were being washed. I don't know how many dogs there were on board as I never counted them. I am not sure how many sheep and pigs as I never counted. The doctor slept in the Surgery – this was in the poop, the corner nearest the main deck. I can't say whether any patients were ever in the Surgery.

Cross examined by Doctor of Ship

I never saw you drunk or under influence of drink. There was a great deal of sickness. The passengers always spoke in terms of praise of the Doctor. I heard that the Doctor went to sleep in the Surgery as he had suspicions of the medical comforts being breached as the bulk head partition was insecure. They were breached once or twice before the Doctor went to sleep there. I heard of a man having been at the Brandy Cask and of its running down between decks. I consider the Doctor conducted himself as a Gentleman throughout the voyage.

By the Council

I think we spoke six vessels and communicated with two.

The Commissioner's report read No. 2

Dr Donald by Doctor of Ship

In the report the Commissioners stated everything the Emigrants chose to say. Nothing was reported unfavourable to the Doctor. I handed in your request for an investigation with the allegations. An investigation was impossible till the emigrants left Quarantine.

Statements of passengers read No. 3

<u>**George Hathaway examined**</u>

My name is George Hathaway. The 'tween decks were clean and scraped about twice a week. They were swept every morning. I can't say whether every portion. The beds aired as often as weather permitted. There was shaving on the line. Neptune made his appearance at night. The shaving was in the morning. I saw some shaved and some ducked a bit. Some paid money to get off. I paid a shilling. I don't remember what they were shaved with. There was tar used. They washed it off. It was scraped off with something but what I don't know. Two of my family were ill in the Hospital. There was a man and his wife in the Hospital at one time. I do not know if there were any others then. The passengers were not mustered on Sunday morning that I know of. My name was not called of a Sunday morning. The provisions were served out on the 'tween decks. There was a Surgery on the Poop. There were berths in the Surgery 3 or 4 I think. There were 7 dogs on board sometimes tied, sometimes loose. They were tied round main hatchway. They were often loose. The decks were washed every morning. The pigs were loose when the pens were being cleaned out. The sheep were sometimes loose. They messed the decks, the dogs constantly where they were tied up, one of the sailors cleaned it up. There was a stench arising from the dogs. The dogs were washed every morning. I got full rations while on board as much as I could eat. I never saw the Doctor worse for liquor. I never saw the Captain worse for liquor. Clothes were constantly hanging from the berths. I did not see Whitelaw shaved on the line. I did not see any one taken by force and shaved. Two of my children were in the Hospital ages 6 and 4. That was before we called at the Cape. They had all the medical comforts that they required. The doctor gave verbal orders for bedding to be aired now and then. The deck was leaky, my berth was a little wet. I had no dog, 5 of the dogs belonged to James Johnston. The dogs were smuggled on board after the Commissioner left the vessel before she sailed. David Hathaway is my son. He is at work. I was asked to sign the petition to the Government, praying for this enquiry, but refused.

John Brown examined

My name is John Brown. I was ill a few days. I was not in the Hospital. I am a married man. My wife was confined on board. The Doctor was not attentive to my wife during her illness. I went twice & Norbury once for him before he came. I saw him myself. I went to the Surgery and found him. He said he would come presently in a quarter of an hour. I waited for an hour then Mr Norbury went. I then went myself and the Doctor and I went down together. That was about an hour between my first going for the Doctor and his coming. I had 3 other children ill at the same time. The doctor was attentive to them except to the eldest. I went to fetch the doctor to him. The doctor said he was too busy then to attend to him. But would come in the morning; he gave them all the same medicine; two of them were taken to the hospital, one died soon after he was taken to the hospital. He was strong enough to walk to the Hospital. There were only my three children in the Hospital at that time. There were six beds in the Hospital. I don't know whether the hospital was full. The hospital was for men and women. I could not say whether men and women were ever there together. I don't think my children got justice done them at the time they were ill. My wife and child were in the hospital. I wanted to stay with my wife and in the Hospital because the nurse didn't understand what she said. They would not let me stay with her because they said she was about to be confined. A man was constantly in the hospital about the time when my wife was confined. He was a passenger constantly there; his name was George Richardson. Robert Wallis, James Walker, James Morton have seen him there. Robert Wallis is a mason working somewhere in the Town. They told me that Richardson was often in the Hospital and wondered I stood it. I have seen the Doctor once worse for drink. He said himself that he had had a glass too much. He said it to Mrs Norbury, myself and Mrs Scott. I suppose the Testimonial to the Doctor was signed by the people themselves, no threats were used that I know of. I declined to sign it myself. I saw shaving on the line. I was compelled to pay to get off myself. It was some time during Forenoon. The first thing I saw was a great piece of canvas tied up by the corners and the hose filling it with water. This was about 8 o'clock in the morning. The Captain and Doctor were not there when I went up. I then helped my wife to dress; the sailors came down with blacked faces, they came to my berth. I don't know how many, 10 or 12. They passed me by them. I cannot say whether all the women were dressed. They came back to me afterward and told me I was wanted on the poop. Some of the sailors were there. I was asked whether I would pay or be shaved. I said I would pay, they said it was 1/6. I only had 1/ which I gave them. A few resisted being shaved. The canvas and water was in front of the poop. The Captain and Doctor were on the poop at the time. The Doctor said he had no feeling for one of the men who was shaved. The shaving lasted some hours. I was looking on about ½ an hour. The Doctor and Captain were there all that time. Some dark stuff was smeared over the face. Scraped off with a piece of old iron. Tumbled heels over head into the water and swilled with water by two men. The hose was not used. My bedding was never wet. I have heard other bedding was wet but never saw it. I got as much food as I required.

[Cross examined] By C.W. Turner.

The child my wife was confined of was a 7 months child.

By the Doctor of the Ship

It was a stormy night when my wife was confined. I don't remember that you were standing on a box in the Surgery with a pot of water in the place and could not find your clothes. You were the worse of Drink that night. I don't recollect that I ever said to you that I had said you had been very kind to my children and that you ought to have dinner given you on shore when we arrived. I saw you encouraging the shaving.

Mrs Scott examined

I am the wife of Andrew Scott. I was in the Hospital occasionally. I was there one night and another part of the night. I recollect the shaving. My husband was not shaved. I saw one shaved. I was on deck. The nurse and her sister and Mrs Brown were in the hospital when I was there. I never saw the Doctor the worse for liquor. I was with Mrs Brown when she was confined. It was a very stormy night so much so that I had to be supported while washing the baby. I never saw any men in the Hospital. I never noticed the sailors below. I was so much taken up with the sick. Dr Dermott and some other Doctor inspected the Emigrants at Gravesend. One child was sent away in the fever. The Doctor had no one to dispense medicine for him that I know of.

By Doctor of the Ship.

You were not drunk when you attended Mrs Brown in her confinement. You said a wave had come into your cabin and you would not come before. You were attentive to her. I have seen you about the ship at all hours in attendance on the sick. A few have a bad feeling against you. I recollect John Whitelaw. I heard you tell the sailors not to interfere with Whitelaw to shave him. James Johnstone is my brother in law. I have seen Johnstone get bottles of wine several times for his child which was sick. Mrs Johnston had a bad feeling against you. She said you had passed 3 times by her child without going to see it. I saw nothing improper in your conduct at any time during the passage. I was with Mrs Norbury when her child died; you were not drunk then. I think if you had had more porter to give the Emigrants they would have been less discontented.

By the Council

I don't recollect hearing the Doctor say he had had a glass too much. I never saw any man in the hospital who was not a patient there, except the brother of the nurse who came now and then to see if she wanted any tea. The nurse was a married woman and lost her husband and child on board. Her sister slept with her after her husband's death.

By Mr Turner

I went backwards and forwards a good deal among the passengers on the passage. I saw no immorality on board.

By the Council

I never saw George Richardson in the hospital.

John Mason examined

My name is John Mason. I recollect the time my wife was confined. It was not a stormy night. The Doctor was the worse for drink. I know it from the way he fell upon my wife. I never saw him worse for liquor at other times. One or two of the sailors were sometimes below. I was not shaved on the line. I did not pay. A few of us would not pay. The Doctor said we ought to pay or be shaved. It was down in my berth, the Doctor went away for a few minutes, when he came back he said he would pay for the porter himself as they were religious persons. I don't know how many paid or how many were shaved. I never saw the Captain worse for liquor. I don't know Richardson. I know Mrs Power. I don't know anything wrong with Mrs Power's sister. I was not in that part of the ship. I don't know of any immorality taking place. I had plenty to eat. The officers were attentive. The Doctor was attentive as far as I saw. I did not sign the Testimonial to the Doctor. The people kept themselves clean. The Doctor told them to clean their berths out. I was in the after part of the ship. I have nothing to complain of the Doctor with the exception of that time he attended my wife at her confinement and when we landed at the Quarantine, my wife fainted and he did not pay any attention to her.

By the Doctor of the Ship

I have no employment at this time. I would have come if I had had employment to give this evidence. I was intimate with Whitelaw. Whitelaw had no bad feeling against you. Andrew Scott, Whitelaw, Robert McKay and Mason besides myself neither paid nor were shaved. I swear you were drunk when you attended my wife. I was married on 1st June. I never heard her say Doctor look at my child. I was quite sure you saw me at Camp Bay when I wanted you to attend to my wife.

Mrs Grainger examined

I had a cabin near the Hospital. I know Mrs Powers (the nurse) also her sister. I know Richardson, he was a friend of Mrs Powers. I know of no impropriety between him and her sister. I was ill onboard. The Doctor was attentive. I got everything I asked for. I never saw him the worse for liquor. There was no want of cleanliness to inconvenience.

By the Doctor of the Ship

You were not drunk the night Norbury's child died. I have never seen you commit anything improper.

By the Council

Mrs Norbury always spoke well of the Doctor on board the ship. I don't know why the passengers have changed in their feeling towards the Doctor since their arrival.

By the Doctor of the Ship

I saw you with Mrs Brown the night of her confinement.

Dr Dermott's Statement

I did not know that shaving was going to take place. I saw no passengers shaved neither did I encourage it. I did not take any active measures to prevent it. I give an unqualified denial to having ever been drunk on the passage. I drank freely of wine and spirits at all hours as I was excessively harassed and overworked. I slept in the Surgery to guard against the medical stores being stolen. I believe that the sickness that prevailed was brought onboard and was aggravated by want of proper ventilation.

Mrs Maclachlan examined

I was Matron and had direct charge of the Single Women. They behaved well. They got rather unmanageable after landing at the Quarantine Station. I cannot explain the change in the feeling of some of the Emigrants towards the Surgeon. There was no immorality on board to my knowledge. I have had considerable experience in the charge of Emigrants. I went out to Melbourne in '56 in the *Nugget* in charge of 200 single women. I think the conduct on board the *Brother's Pride* will bear favourable comparison with that on the *Nugget*.

By the Doctor of the Ship

I think decency and order prevailed on board and the sailors were orderly. I saw you at eleven o'clock the night when Mrs Brown's child was born, it was a very stormy night also at 2 o'clock the following morning you were certainly not drunk at these times. You were strict and firm in your conduct towards the Emigrants. I have seen nothing wrong in your conduct. I have never seen you drunk. I know of no instance of inattentiveness on your part to the Emigrants. Your arrangements were generally good.

By Mr Turner

The rations were ample and regularly served out.

References

1. The Sunderland Site Page 123. at <http://www.searlecanada.org/sunderland/sunderland123.html#1857>
2. What is a Clipper Ship? | Marine Insight. at <http://www.marineinsight.com/marine/life-at-sea/maritime-history/what-is-a-clipper-ship-2/>
3. Barque. *Wikipedia, the free encyclopedia* (2012). at <http://en.wikipedia.org/w/index.php?title=Barque&oldid=509355891>
4. Boultenhouse_Art.pdf. at <http://heritage.tantramar.com/Boultenhouse_Art.pdf>
5. McMillan. at <http://homepages.rootsweb.ancestry.com/~mwi/mcmillan/>
6. A ' Brother's Pride' Emigrant. 4 April 1902. *Bay Of Plenty Times* 2 (1902).
7. Wikipedia contributors. Bahia. *Wikipedia, the free encyclopedia* (2012). at <http://en.wikipedia.org/w/index.php?title=Bahia&oldid=513117022>
8. History of Sackville, New Brunswick which includes a list of ships built there. at <http://www.canadagenweb.org/archives/nb/sackvill.txt>
9. Wikipedia contributors. Packet ship. *Wikipedia, the free encyclopedia* (2012). at <http://en.wikipedia.org/w/index.php?title=Packet_ship&oldid=481049374>
10. Haws, Duncan. Shaw, Savill & Albion. at <http://www.merchantnavyofficers.com/shawsavill.html>
11. Taonga, N. Z. M. for C. and H. T. M. Settlement in the provinces: 1853 to 1870. at <http://www.teara.govt.nz/en/history-of-immigration/5>
12. Shaw, Savill And Albion Company | NZETC. at <http://nzetc.victoria.ac.nz/tm/scholarly/tei-Bre01Whit-t1-body-d5.html>
13. Acland, J. B. A. Shipping papers 'Clontarf, A1': ships regulations and plan. University of Canterbury. Acland. (1855).
14. Costs and Wages in Great Britain. at <http://www.rootsweb.ancestry.com/~irlcar2/wages.htm>
15. Purdy, F. On the Earnings of Agricultural Labourers in England and Wales, 1860. *Journal of the Statistical Society of London* **24**, 328–373 (1861).
16. Life at Sea: Museum Victoria. at <http://museumvictoria.com.au/discoverycentre/websites-mini/journeys-australia/1850s70s/life-at-sea/>
17. Diver, M. *The Voyages of the Clontarf*. (Dornie Publishing Company, 2011).
18. SHIPS REPORTS. Bahia arrival. 21 July 1865. *The Sydney Morning Herald* 8 (1865).
19. WATER POLICE COURT. FRIDAY. 22 July 1865. *The Sydney Morning Herald* 5 (1865).
20. SHIPPING INTELLIGENCE. PORT OF MELBOURNE [BY ELECTRIC TELEGRAPH.] ARRIVED (PORT PHILLIP HEADS.) Brother's Pride. 27 July 1865. *Bendigo Advertiser* 2 (1865).
21. ARRIVED (HOBSON'S BAY). Brother's Pride. 29 July 1865. *Bendigo Advertiser* 2 (1865).
22. POLICE. CITY COURT. MONDAY, AUGUST 28. (Before Mr. Sturt, P.M., and Mr. Sutherland, J.P.)[?] Donald McGregor of Brother's Pride. 29 August 1865. *The Argus* 6 (1865).
23. PUBLIC TELEGRAM. Brother's Pride departs Melbourne. 4 September 1865. *The South Australian Advertiser* 3 (1865).
24. ENGLISH SHIPPING. ARRIVALS. Brother's Pride departs London for Sydney. 17 August 1877. *The Sydney Morning Herald* 4 (1877).
25. Email from Al Smith, Boultenhouse Heritage Centre, Tantramar Heritage Trust. Included details of the Brothers Pride. 21 September 2012.
26. Shipping. Bahia journey summary and Brother's Pride anchors at Camp Bay. 9 December 1863. *Press* 2 (1863).
27. Obituary. - J. M. Cambridge. 7 October 1917. *Press* 9 (1918).
28. Births, Deaths and Marriages Online Search. at <https://www.bdmhistoricalrecords.dia.govt.nz/search/>
29. Mrs J.m. Cambridge. 15 February 1902. *Ashburton Guardian* 2 (1902).
30. Cemetery Record Enquiry John Miles Cambridge. at <http://www.adc.govt.nz/cemeteryRecords/61%5C11.html>
31. Town And Country. John Ross arriving on Bahia. 26 September 1863. *Lyttelton Times* 4 (1863).
32. Marriage. Jeanie Ross. 9 July 1901. *Star* 3 (1901).
33. Personal Items. Mr John Ross retires. 30 August 1902. *Press* 7 (1902).

34. Personal. John Ross death. 17 November 1902. *Star* 3 (1902).
35. Port Chalmers—august 20th. 21 August 1863. *Otago Daily Times* 4 (1863).
36. Ships Loading At London For New Zealand To 23rd May. 31 July 1863. *Southland Times* 2 (1863).
37. Ship Brothers' Pride. An account from H. B. Kirk. 14 December 1893. *Star* 1 (1893).
38. Ship Brother's Pride. Fitzherbert Dermott's account. 29 December 1863. *Press* 2 (1863).
39. Shipping. Brother's Pride list of deaths. 10 December 1863. *Press* 2 (1863).
40. Typhus. *Wikipedia, the free encyclopedia* (2012). at <http://en.wikipedia.org/w/index.php?title=Typhus&oldid=527937098>
41. A. Rose (Immigration) to Provincial Secretary - re control of immigration. Filed with 213 8/1/64, D. McLean letter 6/1/64, 46 6/1/64, 46(1) 6/1/64, 46(2) 1/1/64, 46(3) 6/1/64, 1155 15/12/63, 1155(1) 15/12/63, 1155(2) 15/12/63, 1155(3) 15/12/63, 1168 15/12/63. Report Brothers Pride - no date (R22193437). Archives New Zealand, Christchurch. Agency CAAR. Series 19936. Box CP 48 /. Record No. ICPS 89/1864.
42. The Brother's Pride. John Whitelaw letter to the editor . 5 January 1864. *Lyttelton Times* 5 (1864).
43. Craymer, Alfred William, 1862-1863 Diary of a voyage from England to New Zealand, 5 Dec 1862 - 13 Mar 1863. Alexander Turnbull Library, Reference qMS-0585.
44. The Project Gutenberg eBook of Cruise and Captures of the Alabama, by Albert M. Goodrich. at <ftp://ibiblio.org/pub/docs/books/gutenberg/3/5/1/0/35107/35107-h/35107-h.htm>
45. Resident Magistrates' Court. Breach of the Shipping Act. Capt. Alex Glendinning. 6 February 1864. *Lyttelton Times* 5 (1864).
46. David Carr Diary. Lancashire Witch, 1863. ARC 1993.67. Canterbury Museum, Christchurch.
47. Brother's Pride Passenger List 1863 - Family Search Website. at <https://familysearch.org/pal:/MM9.3.1/TH-266-11693-142055-87?cc=1609792&wc=MMR8-GBS:1902227274>
48. Bahia and Brother's Pride arrives. More than average sickness. 8 December 1863. *Press* 2 (1863).
49. Shipping Intelligence. Arrival of the Bahia and Brother's Pride. 8 December 1863. *Lyttelton Times* 4 (1863).
50. The Brother's Pride and journey summary for Bahia. 12 December 1863. *Lyttelton Times* 4 5 (1863).
51. The Brothers' Pride. Captain should be punished. 11 December 1863. *Press* 2 (1863).
52. The Press. Saturday, December 12, 1863. Brother's Pride in quarantine but health mending. *Press* 2 (1863).
53. Town And Country. Brother's Pride in Camp Bay. 22 December 1863. *Lyttelton Times* 4 (1863).
54. A. Rose (Immigration) to Provincial Secretary - re control of immigration. Filed with 213 8/1/64, D. McLean letter 6/1/64, 46 6/1/64, 46(1) 6/1/64, 46(2) 1/1/64, 46(3) 6/1/64, 1155 15/12/63, 1155(1) 15/12/63, 1155(2) 15/12/63, 1155(3) 15/12/63, 1168 15/12/63. Report Brothers Pride - no date (R22193437). Archives New Zealand, Christchurch. Agency CAAR. Series 19936. Box CP 48 /. Record No. ICPS 89/1864.
55. Canterbury Musical Society. 23 December 1863. *Press* 2 (1863).
56. Shipping Intelligence. Pratique. 26 December 1863. *Lyttelton Times* 4 (1863).
57. The Quarantine Ground In Camp Bay. 5 January 1864. *Lyttelton Times* 5 (1864).
58. The Ship Brothers Pride. 15 December 1893. *Press* 5 (1893).
59. Voice, E. G. *The Voices of the Forest of Dean, Gloucestershire, and their descendants in New Zealand, 1798-1984.* (1984).
60. Christchurch Parish Records. Peterborough Central Library, Christchurch.
61. Finding a tricky birth record - Message board - Trade Me. Son of Thomas Paul and Elizabeth King. at <http://www.trademe.co.nz/Community/MessageBoard/Messages.aspx?id=1324460&topic=40&#p26869749>
62. Resident Magistrates' Court. Regina V. Glendinning. Breach of 21st Section of Marine Board Act, 1862. *Lyttelton Times* 5 (1864).
63. Resident Magistrate's Court. 20 January 1864. *Press* 2 (1864).
64. Lyttelton. Captain Glendinning charged. 4 February 1864. *Press* 2 (1864).
65. A. Rose to Provincial Secretary - Immigration report on Brothers Pride, solicits an inquiry.

117

Filed 1158(1) - 15/12/1863 (R22193193). Agency: CAAR, Series: 19936. Accession: CH287. Box/Item: CP 47 /. Record No.: ICPS 1158A/1863. Archives New Zealand, Christchurch Office.

66. Marshman (Emigration) to Provincial Secretary - gratuities Brothers Pride - 23/10/1863 (R22192834). Agency: CAAR. Series: 19936. Accession: CH287. Box/Item: CP 44 /. Record No. ICPS 690A/1863. Archives New Zealand, Christchurch Office.
67. Armstrong (Immigration) to Provincial Secretary - proceeds of sale of effects of emigrants dead by 'Captain Cook' and 'Brothers Pride' - 3/05/1864 (R22194575). Agency: CAAR. Series: 19936. Accession: CH287. Box/Item: CP 54 /. Record no. ICPS 1414/1864. Archives New Zealand, Christchurch Office.
68. Doctor F. Dermott to Provincial Secretary - re Brothers Pride - 3/02/1864 (R22193620) Agency: CAAR. Series: 19936. Accession: CH287. Box/Item: CP 50 /. Record No. ICPS 327/1864. Christchurch Office of Archives New Zealand.
69. Coroner's Inquest. F. Dermott. 26 February 1872. *West Coast Times* 2 (1872).
70. Death. Fitzherbert Dermott. 22 September 1879. *West Coast Times* 2 (1879).
71. The Late Dr. Dermott. 28 July 1880. *West Coast Times* 2 (1880).
72. Town And Country. Immigration Commissioners' report unfit for publication. 9 January 1864. *Lyttelton Times* 4 (1864).
73. Jane Neuse to J.E. Marsh - refuses to pay passage money 'Brothers Pride' - 11/01/1865 (R22196271) Archives NZ, Christchurch Office [Note surname should be Mewes]. at <http://www.archway.archives.govt.nz/ViewFullItem.do?code=22196271>
74. Shearman (Police) to Provincial Secretary - full details of Christchurch brothels, the ladies connected therewith and of their arrival per ships ?Mystery?, ?Mermaid?, ?Captain Cook?, ?Mary Ann?, ?Lincoln?, ?Blue Jacket?, ?Creswell?, ?Lancashire Witch?, ?Amoor? and ?Ambrosine?, as single emigrants 31/12/1867 (R22198680). Archives NZ, Christchurch Office. at <http://www.archway.archives.govt.nz/ViewFullItem.do?code=22198680>
75. Session 21 - Paper not tabled - Evidence as to conduct of ship 'Brother's Pride', taken before the Executive Council at the Government Buildings. [This unnumbered paper was prepared for tabling, but does not appear to have been tabled, and is not recorded in the Journal of Proceedings] - 15 Jan 1864. (R20592711). Agency, CAAR. Series, 20410. Accession, CH287. Box/Item, CP 610/c. Record no. PPC 1. Archives NZ, Christchurch Office. at <http://www.archway.archives.govt.nz/ViewFullItem.do?code=20592711>
76. Immigration. Brother's Pride mentioned. 2 September 1868. *Timaru Herald* 6 (1868).
77. *Christchurch Parish Records. Peterborough Central Library, Christchurch.*
78. CCC Cemeteries Database Results Summary. at <http://librarydata.christchurch.org.nz/Cemeteries/interment.asp?surname=crosbie&firstname=&year1=&year2=&cemeterycode=-1&plot=7A&block=7>
79. The Orphan Asylum. 10 May 1864. *Lyttelton Times* 5 (1864).
80. Shipping Intelligence. Bahia departs Lyttelton. 23 January 1864. *Lyttelton Times* 4 (1864).
81. Town And Country. Screw Pile Jetty. 10 October 1862. *Lyttelton Times* 4 (1863).
82. Page 3 Advertisements Column 2. Brother's Pride Reunion 21 November 1893. *Star* 3 (1893).
83. Papers Past — Star — 15 December 1893 — BROTHERS' Pride Reunion. Brothers' Pride Reunion. at <http://paperspast.natlib.govt.nz/cgi-bin/paperspast?a=d&cl=search&d=TS18931215.2.10>
84. News Of The Day. Brother's Pride 32nd reunion. 25 November 1895. *Press* 5 (1895).
85. Page 1 Advertisements Column 7. Brother's Pride 40th reunion 5 December 1903. *Press* 1 (1903).
86. Shipmates Re-unite. 11 December 1913. *Press* 4 (1913).
87. Obituary. Robert Anderson. 12 August 1907. *Press* 9 (1907).
88. Templeton | NZETC. at <http://nzetc.victoria.ac.nz/tm/scholarly/tei-Cyc03Cycl-t1-body1-d6-d22.html>
89. Married Sixty Years - Bayliss. 18 December 1943. *Auckland Star* 7 (1943).
90. William Brassington. *Wikipedia, the free encyclopedia* (2012). at <http://en.wikipedia.org/w/index.php?title=William_Brassington&oldid=509221047>
91. Obituary. Alex Burnett. 27 July 1906. *Wairarapa Daily Times* 5 (1906).
92. Part 48 - The Dudley West Midlands line. Collett Family. at <http://www.collettfamilyhistory.net/Part%2048%20-%20The%20Dudley%20West%20Midlands%20Line%20Rev.7.htm>

93. Page 1 Advertisements Column 4. David Dunlop's farm in St Albans. 5 September 1877. *Press* 1 (1877).
94. Deaths. David Dunlop lost infant daughter. 29 September 1880. *Star* 2 (1880).
95. CCC Cemeteries Database Results Summary. David Dunlop. at <http://librarydata.christchurch.org.nz/Cemeteries/interment.asp?surname=dunlop&firstname=david&year1=&year2=>
96. Death. Jeanie Dunlop died. Daughter of David Dunlop. 11 June 1886. *Press* 2 (1886).
97. CCC Cemeteries Database Results Summary. Jeanie Dunlop. at <http://librarydata.christchurch.org.nz/Cemeteries/interment.asp?surname=dunlop&firstname=jeanie&year1=&year2=>
98. Family History research essays. George Edmonds on Brother's Pride. at <http://tapuhi.natlib.govt.nz/cgi-bin/spydus/NAV/GLOBAL/OPHDR/1/244704>
99. Resident Magistrate's Court. William Everett. 27 July 1866. *Press* 2 (1866).
100. Old Colonists | NZETC. John Hanson. at <http://nzetc.victoria.ac.nz/tm/scholarly/tei-Cyc03Cycl-t1-body1-d6-d1-d3.html#name-422289-mention>
101. John Edward HANSON (1842 - 1920). at <http://www.norton.gen.nz/ifamily/HTMLFiles/HTMLFiles_01/John_Edward_HANSON_P157.html>
102. Ninety Years Of Age. Mrs John Futter. 29 December 1936. *Evening Post* 11 (1936).
103. Obituary Mary Ann Futter. 4 September 1941. *Evening Post* 12 (1941).
104. Peter and Denise. BrothersPride. at <http://freepages.genealogy.rootsweb.ancestry.com/~ourstuff/BrothersPride.htm>
105. Old Colonists | NZETC. Mr. W. Irvine. at <http://nzetc.victoria.ac.nz/tm/scholarly/tei-Cyc03Cycl-t1-body1-d6-d49-d3.html#name-422708-mention>
106. Farmers | NZETC. Mr T.S. Johnston. at <http://nzetc.victoria.ac.nz/tm/scholarly/tei-Cyc03Cycl-t1-body1-d6-d71-d2.html>
107. Old Colonists | NZETC. H. B. Kirk. at <http://nzetc.victoria.ac.nz/tm/scholarly/tei-Cyc03Cycl-t1-body1-d7-d1-d46.html#name-423488-mention>
108. ChristchurchStreetNames-A.pdf. at <http://christchurchcitylibraries.com/Heritage/PlaceNames/ChristchurchStreetNames-A.pdf>
109. Obituary. Gordon McConnell. 9 January 1909. *Press* 4 (1909).
110. Obituary. Mrs Alexander McKay. 1 November 1909. *Ashburton Guardian* 3 (1909).
111. Double Hill — (Runs 272, 291, 352, 428, 435-6-7, 446, 459, 460) | NZETC. at <http://nzetc.victoria.ac.nz/tm/scholarly/tei-AclEarl-t1-body-d11-d12.html>
112. New Zealand, South Canterbury Links. Jessie McKay, daughter of Robert McKay. at <http://www.rootsweb.ancestry.com/~nzlscant/links.htm#mackay>
113. Farmers | NZETC. Alexander McKenzie. at <http://nzetc.victoria.ac.nz/tm/scholarly/tei-Cyc03Cycl-t1-body1-d6-d90-d2.html>
114. Town Edition. Death of Alexander McKenzie. 16 November 1915. *Poverty Bay Herald* 6 (1915).
115. Builders And Contractors | NZETC. Robert McMillan. at <http://nzetc.victoria.ac.nz/tm/scholarly/tei-Cyc05Cycl-t1-body1-d3-d22-d5.html#name-432663-mention>
116. Old Colonists — Mr. Colin More, | NZETC. at <http://nzetc.victoria.ac.nz/tm/scholarly/tei-Cyc03Cycl-t1-body1-d4-d24-d3.html>
117. CONCERNING PEOPLE. Elizabeth Petherick. 19 February 1913. *The Register* 6 (1913).
118. Mr J. Powell. 19 September 1913. *Press* 3 (1913).
119. Farmers | NZETC. Frederick Roberts. at <http://nzetc.victoria.ac.nz/tm/scholarly/tei-Cyc03Cycl-t1-body1-d6-d10-d2.html>
120. *A Long Way to County Cavan (Life and Memories of the Rountree/Coleman Clan of New Zealand), by Dallas Rountree and Jo Noble.*
121. Email from Margaret Gilmore regarding Joan Scott. (2013).
122. Scrimshaw, Henry | NZETC. at <http://nzetc.victoria.ac.nz/tm/scholarly/tei-Cyc03Cycl-t1-body1-d3-d43-d7.html#name-421083-mention>
123. Shearman (Police) to Provincial Secretary - full details of Christchurch brothels, the ladies connected therewith and of their arrival per ships ?Mystery?, ?Mermaid?, ?Captain Cook?, ?Mary Ann?, ?Lincoln?, ?Blue Jacket?, ?Creswell?, ?Lancashire Witch?, ?Amoor? and ?Ambrosine?, as single emigrants 31/12/1867 (R22198680). Agency, CAAR; Series,

19936; Accession, CH287; Box/Item CP 93; Record No. ICPS 1880/1867. Archives New Zealand, Christchurch Office.
124. Hannah-papa Blog: Family History (3) Smith Family from Scotland. at <http://yoyogi-cohen.blogspot.co.nz/2007/09/family-history-3-smith-family-from.html>
125. Mr. William John Sparks | NZETC. at <http://nzetc.victoria.ac.nz/tm/scholarly/tei-Cyc03Cycl-t1-body1-d3-d20-d18.html>
126. Mr. Peter Thomson | NZETC. at <http://nzetc.victoria.ac.nz/tm/scholarly/tei-Cyc04Cycl-t1-body1-d7-d61-d69.html>
127. Obituary. James Torrens. *Star* 5 (1897).
128. Page 3 Advertisements Column 2 - Absalom Trigg. 5 January 1870. *Daily Southern Cross* 3 (1870).
129. Email from Lee Moake regarding the Voice family on the Brother's Pride. (2013).
130. The Judges' Award On Drays. James Voice, Wheelwright. 24 November 1873. *Press* 3 (1873).
131. Page 3 Advertisements Column 1. James Voice. 3 April 1882. *Press* 3 (1882).
132. 1900.November.Star.Christchurch.BMD. James Voice death. at <http://homepages.ihug.co.nz/~ashleigh/1870-1908/1900.November.Star.Christchurch.BMD.html>
133. Page 14 Advertisements Column 7. George Voice death. 16 January 1915. *Press* 14 (1915).
134. Dunsandel | NZETC. William Walker. at <http://nzetc.victoria.ac.nz/tm/scholarly/tei-Cyc03Cycl-t1-body1-d6-d49.html>
135. William Walker death notice. 6 September 1893. *The Press*
136. Agnes Walker funeral card. Courtesy of Shona C. Webb.
137. Obituary. John Whitelaw. 10 May 1904. *Press* 8 (1904).
138. News Of The Day. John Whitelaw. 12 May 1904. *Press* 4 (1904).
139. Accidents And Fatalities. - William Woodhouse. 6 June 1898. *Star* 1 (1898).
140. Shipping Intelligence. Bahia passengers listed. 10 December 1863. *Lyttelton Times* 4 (1863).
141. *Voice Family Record 1798-1980* by Edna Gyde, Jean Sloan, Freda Hammersley, Hilda Coppard.
142. Criminal Calendar. Niel Beaton charged with larceny. 3 October 1873. *Daily Southern Cross* 3 (1873).

View from Camp Bay, 2013 (Belinda Lansley)

www.ingramcontent.com/pod-product-compliance
Lightning Source LLC
Chambersburg PA
CBHW050650160426
43194CB00010B/1884